Helen Cross

grow cook inspire

Growing and cooking for a
healthier mind and planet

Illustrations by Ruth Craddock

Foreword by Dr James Morton

g

First published in the UK in 2023 by Grow Cook Inspire.

ISBN: 978-1-3999-5080-0

Design and page layout: Raspberry Creative Type, Edinburgh
Photography: Helen Cross
Illustrations: Ruth Craddock
Foreword: Dr James Morton
Editing and proof reading: Lucy Gillmore & Mandy Bradshaw

Printed and bound in Great Britain by Bell & Bain LTD, Glasgow

Instagram @grow_cook_inspire

www.growcookinspire.com

£20.00

For Otto, Reuben and Ivor. My original three seedlings growing up fast.

"The love of gardening is a seed that once sown never dies, but grows to the enduring happiness that the love of gardening gives."

Gertrude Jekyll

Contents...

Swallowtail
Butterfly

Foreword

18 months ago, I lived in a tiny two-bedroom mews house in urban Glasgow. My garden composed of a couple of big pots plonked next to our front door, that opened straight onto our asphalt lane. I watered and overwatered them religiously. With no idea of what to expect, we were desperate to move into a forever home with a garden, and to start laying down some roots.

Then, a message from Helen about a house that came up for sale just a few doors down from her own. One thing, of course, led to the next, and soon our little family lived in a big old house with a wraparound garden, innumerable fruit trees and 8-foot overgrown borders. This garden was once loved, but recently left to go wild. "Not knowing where to start" would be an understatement.

I'm privileged to have both Helen as a friend brimming with ideas and recommendations, but also to have her as a neighbour: her own garden and the inspiration it provides is so close at hand. I know what to plant – I know what works – around an exceptionally busy life with little kids taking up every waking minute, because Helen has done it already. She might even have some seeds for me if I'm lucky.

Her enthusiasm is infectious. Within months of moving in, I had raised beds full of vegetables. I knew how to care for my fruit trees, my roses bloomed, and the long-suppressed perennials and biennials were allowed to flourish, as the soil was respected, and the weeds and roots and suckers were gradually pulled out.

My two-year-old daughter, too – once upon a time fed up after minutes out in the cold and wet of Glasgow – soon started to ask to go outside into the garden. "Want to go digging, Daddy." "Want to find worms." Her enthusiasm bolstered by harvesting her new

potatoes that we'd planted together a few months before, then cooking them and serving them simply with fresh herbs and butter. We even decorated them, on Helen's recommendation, with nasturtium flowers, grown from seeds she'd donated.

As our family grows, so do our plants and our passion for gardening. I hope this is something that bonds us, and remains a passion, for life. In fact, I can't see how it won't be. If you can draw upon the words in this book, written with the same love and excitement for gardening and cooking that I see in Helen every day, then I can guarantee you'll succumb to her enthusiasm. You too can grow and cook and inspire others to do the same.

Dr James Morton, author, baker, and newly obsessed gardener

Introduction

In March 2020, our fast-paced lives came to a standstill. In a flash overnight, cars vanished from the roads, aeroplanes were erased from the skies and people retreated into their homes. Our life, as we had come to know it, changed in a heartbeat.

We were forced to stay at home and our gardens, balconies and windowsills provided a space to nurture hope with each seed planted. The green spaces that surrounded our homes were placed on a pedestal. The sounds of engines were replaced with birdsong, which had always been there, but had been drowned out by the way we now live. We became more aware of our natural surroundings. As the seasons changed, small differences were magnified and there was beauty in everyday things; the first tulips emerging from hibernation, the robin appearing at the kitchen window, and the aroma of wild garlic in the nearby woods was more pungent than I can ever remember.

I watched our small, city, terraced garden evolve from a blank canvas into a glorious sanctuary for bees and butterflies. I revelled in growing pumpkins and peas and so much more with my three young boys, from tiny seeds sown in yoghurt tubs on our kitchen windowsill. My goal was not to make us self-sufficient, that would never be possible. The reality was – and still is – small handfuls of strawberries here, tablespoons of peas there and enough potatoes for four or five proper good suppers.

Our garden is measured in feet rather than acres, there is no grand glasshouse, walled kitchen garden or an orchard brimming with heritage fruit trees. Nevertheless, our garden, a very typical long, narrow, mid-terrace, urban garden, became a place to grow not only plants and flowers but to grow as people too.

The picture painted above sounds idyllic, except there was a global pandemic in the background. Separated from friends and family, anxiety and fear escalated due to the unknown. Loved ones died and life seemed out of control.

The garden and kitchen, however, were areas of our life we could control, to some extent. Cooking and growing food is something most of us take for granted. Both became so much more. They are activities which, although simple, can be so enriching for both the body and the mind. Each plant dug into the ground and each meal cooked provided a focus – a distraction and an escape. Nature is in our DNA. We are hunter-gatherers. However, the way we now live has dissolved this connection with nature. Built-up urban areas are a new phenomenon given how long we have lived on planet Earth. The consequences are dire for both our mental and physical health, the path we choose to create for our children to follow and the environment we live in.

The purpose of this book is not to preach. In no way am I perfect, and I don't have all the answers. I just want seasonal cooking, eating, and gardening with nature at its core to become more mainstream. Part of our daily lives at home and within our schools, nurseries, and the wider community. Young people are hugely aware of environmental issues. Encouraging and supporting them to engage with cooking and growing their own will help them to flourish further. Gardening is also a powerful tool to harness a positive, practical, and creative interest in conservation, science, and environmentalism. With this in mind, I have included activities to help inspire more of us to recycle in the garden and think of nature as the beating heart of our green spaces at home and beyond.

As well as the climate crisis, a mental health crisis is sweeping across the UK. The pandemic and the cost-of-living crisis has taken a huge toll on adult's and young people's mental health, regardless of how resilient we think we are, especially our children. What's more, those who were suffering from mental health issues before the pandemic saw these problems escalate. Loneliness among young people has been a huge trigger, with nine out of 10 young people believing loneliness has contributed to poor mental health due to the pandemic.

It is vital we support the next generation and ourselves. This is something I believe both gardening and cooking can help with, and I am backed up by the science: a Danish study found that just 10 weeks of gardening had the same effect as 10 weeks of cognitive behavioural therapy. This is just one of many examples. I can relate fully to the debilitating impact anxiety and depression can have on your own life and on the life of those around you. I have long suffered from anxiety, which evolved into an eating disorder in my late teens and early twenties. Following the birth of my first child I suffered from post-natal depression and anxiety, which continued to hound me during my next two pregnancies, picked up pace again through the pandemic and continues to strangle me.

Like so many, I was stuck at home with three small children as my husband worked long shifts as an NHS doctor. My mind went into overdrive during this period. I was diagnosed with severe health anxiety, which escalated off the scale. The path ahead looked bleak. I didn't recognise myself at times and neither did my friends or family.

I did, however, find an escape from the thoughts in my head within our garden, and then our kitchen. The recipes and projects within *Grow Cook Inspire* capture a glimmer of the light we found during a very dark period.

This book is meant as a companion for parents, grandparents, carers, and teachers to share with children. It will empower you to learn together and increase your confidence in the kitchen and garden. It is also a call-to-arms, to highlight that we all have a responsibility to look after our environment. This book will provide the tools and knowledge to allow everyone to play their part, no matter how big or small. It doesn't have to be perfect.

I will guide you and your children to grow fruits, vegetables, and herbs, whether you're growing from a balcony, in pots or have a garden. I provide top tips, guidance on growing, fun facts and recipes for every ingredient along with advice on how to prevent food waste. There is also a guide to safe foraging with children and recipes, as well as fun projects to encourage everyone to embrace the wilder side of gardening and cut loose from outdated practices, which are strangling our environment.

Both gardening and cooking must not be put on the back burner but looked at through a different lens. Both are a way of finding calm and purpose in an otherwise chaotic, and a sometimes confusing and changing world.

Many can relate to feeling rudderless. You may feel you are stumbling through life in the dark with no direction or agency, but gardening and cooking provide purpose, as well as hope and power. They encourage and cultivate patience, curiosity, kindness, and creativity; essential qualities to explore early on in life. Above all, both our green spaces and our kitchens are playgrounds. They are places where we can learn together but also have fun.

By marrying gardening, cooking, and foraging with children together into one comprehensive book, I want to highlight the importance of reconnecting with nature for the long term. Children have a short attention span, so the recipes and projects must be practical and fit in around family and life. There are moments of brilliance and joy when cooking and gardening with children but let's take off the rose-tinted glasses and get real for a moment.

There will be mess, tears and things not turning out as you had hoped. This is reality not Instagram. I want to dispel the idea that everything must be 'just so' and embrace the failures and the fact your tomatoes might not get off the starting blocks. It is still fun to have a go and in fact it is how we learn and keep learning, and why it will evolve into an obsession. Trust me on this. It will become an addiction you will want to share with everyone and anyone, regardless of whether they want to listen or not.

Sticky fingers, flour on the floor, muddy feet and hands are all signs of a good time. There are no carefully curated gardens or show home kitchens on my patch, but that makes them more inviting. Through the pages of *Grow Cook Inspire* I want to invite you into our home and allow you to perfectly, imperfectly, cook and garden along with us. Everyone is welcome.

Now let's kick on as I show you why we could all do with gardening and cooking seasonally a little more, for our health and the health of the environment. Step this way.

Lettuce

Pumpkin

Carrots

Vitamin G...

Horticultural therapy and mindful gardening are two popular buzz phrases, which have been making headlines and for good reason. Green spaces, nature and gardening have the power to make us feel better, ground us, and help us to find calm when there is a tidal wave of worry crashing around us. They have the power to heal, soothe and repair. The same benefits can also be derived from cooking. The perfect pairing when it comes to looking after ourselves and those around us.

In recent years the taboos and stigmas surrounding mental health have been slowly tackled and broken down to a large extent. As a result, more people have been willing to come forward and talk about how gardening has supported them with their own mental health and the therapeutic benefits they have gained from nature.

As humans we spend a lot of time inside our heads. We're frequently looking ahead to the future or reflecting on the past. Rarely are we in the moment and enjoying the present. Gardening, however, has the power to pull you into the present moment and all other thoughts are banished. This is the joy of gardening and cooking for that matter. It's powerful medicine for the mind and soul as well as the planet.

For tired, frazzled minds and anxious over thinkers, me included, sowing seeds, gently stirring a pot of soup, grating cheese, or simply dicing carrots can help overpowering thoughts melt away into the abyss. You're immersed in the moment when out in the garden or in the kitchen. Your focus is not what has to be done next but what you're creating or nurturing at that time. By slowing down and engaging with the processes and tuning into the seasons we begin to relax. Our heart rate slows down as does our breathing. It's soothing.

Not only is our environment facing unprecedented challenges, but our mental health is also struggling, with 1 in 4 suffering from a mental health illness. As a result of the pandemic the number of young people prescribed antidepressants has increased, while waiting times for appropriate psychological support have also grown. Bereavement, isolation, loss of motivation, and financial hardship have magnified an already terrifying problem.

Just one of these would easily trigger a mental health illness, but many have been confronted by more than one at the same time. The ingredients for the perfect mental health storm. One which has been building over time, confronting an NHS already at breaking point unable to meet the growing demand due to overstretched and underfunded services.

NHS figures, analysed by The Royal College of Physicians published in April 2021 highlighted 80,226 children and young people were referred to mental health services between April 2020 and December 2020, up by 28% on 2019. This number had been increasing over the last five years. With long waiting lists for services, the immediate alternative has been the prescription of antidepressants.

Access to green space and gardening won't remedy all mental health issues but there is strong evidence to suggest both can complement medication and therapy, helping to ease a problem crippling so many and robbing them of their lives.

I have experienced first-hand the impact anxiety and depression can have on my own life and those around me. While on the surface it may appear that I am calm and in control I often feel like I am drowning.

The black dog has long lurked at my door. He comes out of the shadows from nowhere and attacks with devastating consequences. He leaves me feeling hopeless, alone, and frightened. It's debilitating and all consuming. It feels like I may never escape its clutches. Medication and therapy have helped hugely and continue to do so, but my garden has played a pivotal role and is part of my tool kit.

As a mother of young children, you can often feel isolated, alone and that your needs fall to the bottom of the pile and never get the attention they deserve or indeed really need. Your sense of self also vanishes. The day is not yours any longer, but scheduled around school and nursery, after school clubs, homework, playdates, tantrums, and bedtime routines. The pandemic brought new challenges, a lack of human contact, terrifying headlines and the unknown of what was to come. For those predisposed to worry, anxiety and depression this was a dangerous cocktail.

What lay in the garden was a strategy to help when things got dark. Peace, a connection with nature, the reassurance of seasons unravelling as they should when they should and the growth and life that the garden held within her boundaries. When I really struggled to fight the thoughts in my head, which were crushing me and crushing those around me, I forced myself outside. I became detached form the pain of the anxiety.

While some people run, lift weights, or even paint I sow seeds to search for hope and new beginnings. I weed to distract myself from the noise in my head. The soil provides comfort, something that many mothers and women for that matter have done for generations. If I look at my own mother and grandmother, they too have taken comfort in gardening in difficult times. I strongly believe regular exposure to nature from an early age could go a long way to help extinguish the flames of our current mental health crisis.

Gardening provides purpose and structure because there is a living thing reliant upon your care. You begin to take a sense of pride and share your knowledge amongst others. You're constantly learning new things, building yourself up and growing in confidence, and your sense of awareness around you grows. You notice the leaves changing colour, the birds coming to the bird feeder and droplets of water on petals after the rain.

Noticing these small moments can help you escape overwhelming and intrusive thoughts that stop you from doing what you love and spending time with people you care for. To have access to green space on your doorstep should never be taken for granted.

So, what is Vitamin G? We all know we're meant to get a daily dose of Vitamin C and Vitamin D, but the science also highlights a daily dose of Vitamin G (Green) can go a long way to help improve our mental and physical wellbeing, by easing anxiety and depression, reducing blood pressure, managing stress, and helping us to live a longer and healthier life. It has been said that gardening will add years to your life and life to your years. It may seem like a pithy one liner, but it speaks to me.

But why and how? Surely it must be more than just hugging a tree, weeding, and growing carrots. Well, even just a few moments of exposure to nature from a window or a walk around the park can help boost your mood. However, what is extraordinary is that exposure to the soil exposes us to beneficial microbes, boosting our immune system. The bacteria type Mycobacterium vaccae stimulates the release of serotonin, otherwise known as the happy hormone, into the brain, improving mental health. Making us feel happier in essence.

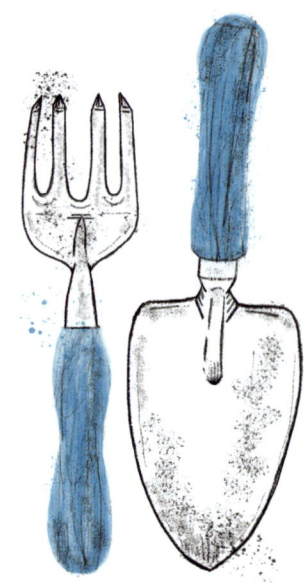

People who love to garden and grow also love to share their knowledge. Connecting with people, whether friends, your neighbour over the garden fence or people within a gardening club, will improve self-esteem and confidence and reduce loneliness.

Gardening and cooking encourage us to experiment, persevere and be patient. Everyone makes mistakes. It's through mistakes we learn. Gardening also evokes a sense of wonder and it's that wonder that draws us in and keeps us engaged. It's why we keep on sowing and growing year after year.

The repetitive nature of something like weeding or sowing seeds is also meditative, helping to relax, restore and recharge tired minds. We have an innate affinity to the natural world but over time we have grown apart. Our mental health and the health of our environment has declined. Gardeners can play a huge role in supporting the environment through more sustainable practices and, in turn, their health will be in much better shape too.

For children especially, growing their own food will provide a real sense of achievement and improve self-esteem and confidence. It can go a long way towards improving engagement, concentration and reducing aggressive behaviours, while also promoting healthy living.

Gardening provides a new outlet to focus on, a safe place to retreat without judgement. There is no baggage, which may come with school or other extracurricular activities.

It involves aerobic activity and being outside is calming. It's a space to be free and creative and let your personality shine bright. I compare gardening to art. Whether you have a big space or you're growing in a pot, what you decide to grow should reflect you.

It's a blank canvas and you should be able to express yourself freely. That is liberating and empowering and can go a long way towards improving our mental health.

I'm not a trained horticulturist. I studied history, but I do want to share my obsession. Once you've caught the bug, you'll understand. You get twitchy around January or February, eager to sow seeds. You know it's too early but having scanned the seed catalogues, despite having a bursting seed box, you spend a small fortune on seeds and sow them far too early.

The first thing you check in the morning before you even reach for the coffee, are your seedlings, just in case they have grown a tiny bit more since the last time you looked. You put off going on holiday for more than two days, as your babies in your veg patch need your attention.

For those who strive for perfection, gardening is a great way to knock that trait on the head. Perfection can never be achieved. Tyrant slugs will put pay to that, as will hungry squirrels' intent on eating every spring bulb planted, and don't forget the weather! However, it's because of this we keep going and keep persevering. It's a healthy addiction and one that will act as a salve during turbulent times, keeping us grounded and anchored in the moment.

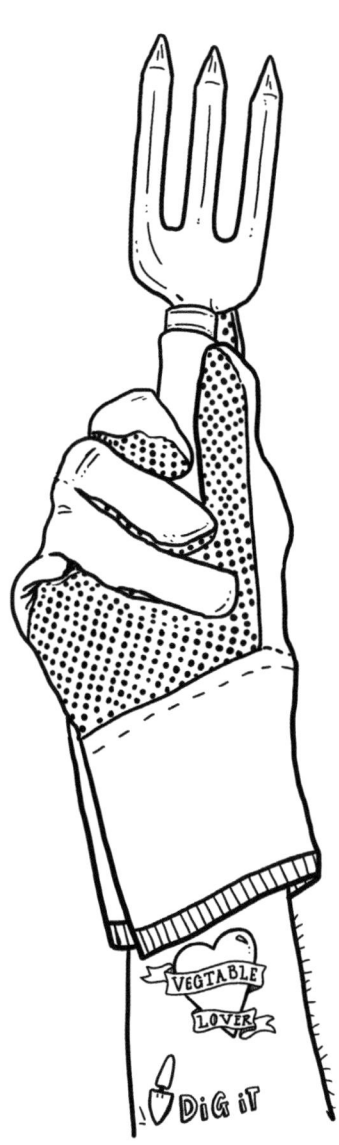

Creative ideas to get growing...

The most natural way to get children of all ages into the garden and into the kitchen is to let them explore for themselves. They'll watch what you're doing and soak it all up without even realising. They'll be happy to follow you about in the garden or simply sit down and dig in the mud, looking for worms. It doesn't need to be structured.

Similarly if you let them pull up a seat while you're cooking supper, rather than making the kitchen a forbidden adult only place, they'll happily chop, stir and no doubt give things a taste.

Encouraging them to wash the dishes is also a great starting point. Although it may be questionable as to how many dishes get washed, what child doesn't love warm soapy water? Exposure is key if you want to spark an interest.

Over the next few pages, I've jotted down a few creative ideas, which may help you to get started in the garden with your mini green fingered crusaders. It doesn't have to be all about sowing seeds and harvesting potatoes from the outset and you don't need to have a garden either.

1. Who doesn't love a *sunflower race*? With each seed sown into a yoghurt tub, I get a sense the race towards the heady days of summer is under way, as the seeds nuzzle down under the compost, preparing themselves before the starting gun is fired. They are, in my humble opinion, the best flower to grow with children. Towering high above everything and everyone else. They are bright, brash, and bold, the epitome of joy. What's more bees love them, and they're a valuable source of food for birds during the last stretch of summer into early autumn.

For best results sow in small tubs from April and then pot on into bigger pots or transplant into the ground when more established. Or you can sow them straight into the ground after the last frost. We've found sunflowers grown straight into the ground are often stronger in the long run. My top tip for super tall sunflowers is sheep manure, giving them an extra edge – will guarantee the need for an extra-long measuring tape!

2. *Edible flowers* are a must. Use them for decorating cakes, biscuits, scatter them through salads or freeze into ice cubes to add a little extra jazz to summertime drinks. My favourites are nasturtiums, calendula, violas and lavender, which can all be grown from seed.

3. If like me you are forever taking photos of your flowers and filling up your camera roll, press them instead. It had been our intention to create a monthly diary of *pressed flowers*, selecting our star picks, but we never quite got round to it. However on the occasion we did pick and press flowers, we put them in frames, made beautiful cards and book marks. The best bit, you don't even need a flower press.

Simply pick the flowers and place between two sheets of baking paper, sandwiched between the pages of a big book, usually a cookbook. We then take heftier cookbooks and place them on top to make sure they are pressed down good and proper. Leave for four to six weeks, resisting the temptation to peek, before removing them.

4. Even on colder days your creativity doesn't have to *freeze* and come to a standstill, as much as you may want to curl up under a duvet. Fill cupcake baking trays with water, add leaves and berries from the garden and place a piece of string in each one, allowing a length to be out of the water. Leave outside overnight to freeze. Remove the next day and hang from branches. They will glisten in the sunlight and slowly melt.

5. If you collect *seed and flower catalogues* for inspiration, why not use them to get crafty. All you need is a catalogue, a piece of paper, scissors, and some glue. Let children design their own garden and colour scheme by cutting out and creating a collage. You may even discover you have a new up and coming designer in your midst.

6. Find *a plant which shares its name* with someone in your family. Pictured right is a dahlia called 'Otto's Thrill' and a quick Google search will throw up some suggestions to match names which mean something to you. I've also discovered a rose called 'Ivor' and a blackberry bush that shares its name with 'Reuben'. So, everyone is happy.

7. Encourage a *daily diary* during one of the summer months and count how many butterflies, bees and other pollinators and insects you can spot, whether in your own garden or while out for a walk. Notice which plants different species are attracted to the most. You could also repeat at the start of autumn and spring and notice the differences.

8. Get children involved from the *very beginning* of the growing process. It still blows my mind that a tiny seed planted in May will produce huge pumpkins in October. Children will get a huge sense of achievement from being involved in the whole journey.

9. *Collecting and saving seeds* is addictive and, as I thrive on being thrifty, it is something I really enjoy doing. Seed – collecting is also an important and sustainable habit to get good at from an early age. In fact, there is nothing better than growing your own flowers from seed, unless of course you've also collected the seed that you have sown to grow them.

It's also relatively easy to do and some of the easiest seeds to collect are nasturtiums, sweet peas, calendula, cornflowers, sunflowers, and poppies. My favourites are cornflower seeds, which look like tiny paint brushes.

Once your flowers have bloomed and the seed head has turned brown, wait for a dry day, before collecting the seed heads. Let them dry for a week. Sift through the chaff and remove the seeds, storing them in a paper envelope for the next growing season.

You could even arrange a seed swap or set up a school seed shop. They make great gifts, stocking fillers or even an alternative to crackers on the Christmas dinner table. Just remember to label correctly to avoid any mishaps.

10. Even if you don't have your own outdoor space, *collecting succulents or any type of house plant* is a great way to start growing an interest in all thing's plants. There is something quite intriguing about these mesmerising plants, which draw the attention of children, especially the prickly cacti. What's more, you don't have to travel to far-flung places to kick off your collection as they can be found easily in supermarkets, DIY stores and garden centres.

11. Just as it's important to give children space in the kitchen, it's also important to give them space in the garden. This could be their own small patch to plant whatever they like, or they may just want to dig holes. You could give them their own raised bed if space permits or give them a corner to create their own *fairy or dinosaur garden,* as we've done. The corner at the bottom of our garden was just dirt and bricks. The boys sowed a mixture of wildflower and sunflower seeds and added branches and bricks to create a dinosaur jungle. Only a lack of imagination will restrict what can be achieved.

180g plain flour

55g caster sugar

125g unsalted butter, softened

2 tsp orange blossom

One good handful of edible flowers such as lavender, nasturtiums, calendula, or cornflowers

Orange blossom shortbread

This is such a fun activity to do with children and makes for a lovely gift. However, whenever baking with children, in my experience, not that much of the dough will make it into the oven.

You can but try – or your children may be far better behaved than mine! In which case, you'll have lots to give away.

1. Preheat the oven to 180C and line one large baking tray or two smaller baking trays with baking paper.

2. In a food mixer combine the sugar and the butter and then add in the flour and the orange blossom. Mix it all together.

3. Turn the dough out onto a floured surface and, using a rolling pin, roll out the dough. Using a cookie cutter, cut out as many biscuit shapes as possible until you have used up all the dough.

4. Place on the tray. Prick with a fork and then gently press an edible flower on to each. Cover with baking paper and gently roll over the dough and the flowers with a rolling pin. Lift the baking paper away.

5. Bake in the oven for 10 -12 minutes or until slightly golden in colour, then remove from the oven.

Sweet peas are my number one cut flower to grow at home and are great to grow with children. From sowing to harvesting, you can illustrate the whole journey from start to finish very easily.

12. Few things make me happier than stepping outside into the garden to *pick and create my own bouquet of flowers, or, in our case, jam jars of flowers*, for friends and family. Home-grown flowers are up there with a big slab of gooey melt-in-your-mouth chocolate brownies. In fact, given together they'd be the ultimate gift. Growing your own cut flowers is a fantastic way to create jam jars of joy for others and home-grown cut flowers are also a great way to reduce your carbon footprint.

A bouquet of flowers grown in the UK produces 95% fewer carbon emissions than a bouquet of flowers grown in the Netherlands. You don't even have to give them away. Growing your own cut flowers is a great way to bring the outdoors indoors – an instant mood lifter.

Sweet peas, dahlias, cosmos, sunflowers, and roses are my top five favourite cut flowers to grow at home and all can be grown in containers. During the winter months, once alliums, poppies and hydrangeas have gone over, they make great dried flower displays and can be added to wreaths.

Throughout lockdown the boys and I were constantly making posies of flowers which we would collect from the garden or from the hedgerows in our back lane. I have a habit of collecting jam jars and can never bring myself to recycle them, so my collection serves me well. Our little jars of colour and scent would be left on the doorsteps of neighbours and friends to help lift spirits in time of sorrow, loss, birthdays, anniversaries or just because.

Not only are you bringing happiness to someone else, but you benefit from the feel-good factor of giving something you have grown and cared for as a gift. Children take huge pride in things they have created from scratch. We even created our very own doorstep shop selling a rainbow of colourful jars bursting with flowers in high summer.

The perfect cut flower to get children started must be *sweet peas,* the star of any cottage garden and easy to grow from seed. You can also save the seed from the pods once they have gone over and turned brown. Start sowing in January through to March for a continuous supply of these heavenly scented romantic flowers, which are the icon of any cut flower garden. Although you can plant the seedlings into the ground I prefer to grow them in pots. The bigger and deeper the pot the better. By sowing sweet pea seeds during the winter when it's cold, you'll create a plant that has strong roots and it will be far more robust and flower for longer. That's the theory anyway.

Just some of our home-grown cut flowers gifted to friends and family.

How to grow sweet peas from February.

1. Fill toilet roll tubes with peat-free compost and sow two seeds per tube and cover with a layer of more compost.

2. Firm the surface and place the tubes in an old ice cream tub and water well. Don't let them dry out. Keep well-watered.

3. Place on a warm windowsill and watch them germinate.

4. Pinch out the top of the seedlings to three to four leaves. This will encourage several strong flower stems for each sweet pea plant. Before planting out from April, you will have to harden them off for a couple of weeks outside, bringing them inside at night.

5. Arrange at least 7 or 8 seedlings in a large pot from late April, filled with peat free compost. Create a wigwam from small tree branches and sticks. The tendrils will cling onto the wigwam, but you will have to use some garden twine to tie them up and ensure they climb onwards and upwards.

6. When they begin to flower the key is to pick and pick. The more you cut, the more the plant will flower, giving you flowers all summer long.

7. My kids also love spotting and cutting off the excess tendrils. Cutting these off makes sure the plant is directing its energy towards producing more flowers. But don't get too hung up about that.

8. Finally, fill jam jars with your own home-grown flowers.

HOW TO MAKE A SEED STARTING POT!

ALL you need is Scissors, Loo Roll, Soil, seeds

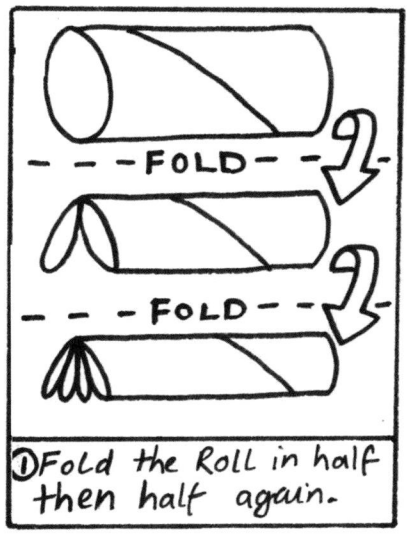

① Fold the Roll in half then half again.

② Unfold and cut 4 even slits on each side.

③ Gently fold in slits to make a flat base.

④ Turn over, fill with soil & plant your seed

⑤ Remember to spray your plant each day.

⑥ You can plant the Loo Roll with the Plant.

And finally...

When it comes to **labelling** plants, you can also get creative. We eat a lot of ice lollies in our house, so we save the sticks and reuse them for identifying seedlings. Wooden cutlery is also great to use to identify vegetables in the veg patch and illustrates the patch-to-plate message when growing with children.

My favourite plant markers are roof slates that I find in local skips. Using acrylic marker pens you can have lots of fun designing plant labels.

Old roof slates make for great plant markers

The Soil...

Respect & regenerate the soil

What goes on beneath our feet is just as important, if not more important, than what is happening up above. Life is dependent on soil. It's as alive as the plants and crops we grow in it. In fact, there are more microorganisms in a teaspoon of healthy soil than there are people on Earth.

Made up of minerals, air, water as well as dead and alive organic materials, it provides plants with a strong foundation, allowing roots to become established and providing the nutrients they need to grow and thrive. Soil also filters rainwater and regulates excess water, which causes flooding. More soil and planting and less concreted driveways and fake grass, please.

With awareness of climate change growing every day, our interest in soil health is also growing. Not only does it store carbon, if our soil is healthy, our plants, fruits and vegetables will also be healthy. A staggering 95% of food is derived from the soil beneath our feet. Healthy soil is paramount for nutrient dense crops, yet the UN has said a third of the world's top layer of soil is endangered. A worrying statistic and one that should encourage us to respect and regenerate soil and be more aware of the direct connection between it and the food we eat.

There are a few simple things we can all do to help make a positive impact and improve our soil rather than erode it:

1. Compost all organic waste if you have space. Dealing with green waste is to be encouraged. Avoid discarded garden and food waste from being sent to landfill where it rots and produces methane, a potent greenhouse gas. About 15 million tonnes of household food waste is produced in the UK each year. According to the charity Garden Organic, one home compost bin can divert around 150 kg of waste from landfill each year.

2. Mulch your veggie patch, flower beds, and young trees. This will boost soil health, lock in moisture, and suppress weeds. You can also use leaf mould or even your old compost from containers to do this, minimising waste. It's cheap and sustainable. I often reuse the old compost from our potato containers.

3. Try 'no-dig gardening'. Digging damages soil health and can result in organic matter turning into carbon dioxide. Plus, you'll save your back!

4. Recycle cardboard by shredding it into the compost heap or laying it on the ground to suppress weeds. Soak it with water and then add a good layer of compost on top, ready for planting.

5. Avoid compost containing peat. Extracting peat from peat bogs which have taken hundreds of years to form releases carbon dioxide into the atmosphere. Peat bogs do an excellent job locking in carbon dioxide and are a vital habitat for wildlife. Always buy peat-free compost and if possible, befriend a local farmer or someone who runs a riding school so you can access well-rotted farm manure for free. Your sunflowers and pumpkins will thank you. Trust me!

A quick "how to" guide to composting

Composting is a fascinating way to teach children how they can convert waste into nutrient rich soil, which is also sustainable and, if you dig down deep enough, you can discover more about garden wildlife by unearthing worms and other fascinating insects. Who doesn't love a wiggly worm or a creepy crawly in the garden?

For those who have never attempted to compost, it can seem daunting and complicated. This need not be the case. With a little help and guidance, more of us can create our own 'black gold' whether at home or at school, which is more sustainable and cheaper than using shop-bought compost, which also comes in plastic bags.

Are you ready?

Why compost? It's an environmentally friendly way of dealing with garden and kitchen waste, which will enrich and improve soil for free! I keep an old ice cream tub by the sink for the kitchen scraps, which can then be put into the garden compost bin. An easy reminder for me and the rest of the household and a good habit to get into.

Where do we put it? Position your compost bin in a shady area with an earth base to allow drainage and to access the soil organisms, who do all the heavy lifting and break down the kitchen and garden waste. You can make one out of pallets or buy one online or in garden centres – they look a bit like something from Dr Who.

What can we compost? Ideally your compost heap should be made up of a good mixture of nitrogen-rich green material and carbon-based brown material. Aim roughly for around two-thirds of green material in the shape of vegetable peelings, fruit waste, contents of tea bags, coffee granules, annual weeds, and soft green grass clippings. This will help feed microorganisms, which are the essential cog in the decomposition wheel. The rest should be a mixture of woody brown material, wood chippings, paper, cardboard, straw, or dead leaves. Don't let one material dominate.

What's next? Turn the compost using a fork at least once a month. This will add air, which helps the composting to take place. Keep it moist in dry weather but don't let it get too wet.

When will it be ready? It will take a good year to make a rich dark, crumbly compost. It will be worth the wait and in the meantime buy peat-free compost.

What should I not compost? Bones, meat and fish scraps, dairy fats, oils, plants treated with pesticides or diseased plants, dog, or cat waste.

From plot to plate...

Herbs

No growing endeavour, or meal for that matter, is complete without fresh herbs. They are much more than just a garnish. Herbs make dishes sing and are a feast for all the senses. Even the smallest of gardens can make room for a pot or two of home-grown magic, which can be grown from seed or bought as small plug plants.

Growing herbs is also a great introduction to growing your own, giving you a taste of what is very likely to become an obsession. You can grow them on your kitchen windowsill in a tin can, in a window box or a pot at the back door. You'll be guaranteed an instant hit of freshness you just don't get from a plastic bag of shop bought herbs.

But why bother when you can go into a supermarket and pick some up quickly without all the faff? Well, there are several very good reasons why growing your own herbs is so much better for you and the planet.

Firstly, the varieties you'll find in a supermarket are nothing compared to what you can grow at home. There are thought to be between 50 and 150 different varieties of basil alone. Why stop at just Sweet Basil when you could explore growing Mammoth Basil, Thai Sweet Basil, Lime Basil or even Cinnamon Basil to name just a few.

The same can be said for mint. There are over 600 varieties of mint, from chocolate mint and Strawberry Mint to Pineapple Mint. The options are endless. All herbs can be grown in containers and in fact mint should always be grown in a container as it will spread like wildfire if not contained.

You'll also reduce the amount of plastic you bring home if you grow your own rather than buying from the supermarket. It's cheaper and healthier and every meal will get an instant lift. Herbs can transform a simple plate of spuds into something much more sublime and your roast dinners will be the talk of the town.

Like growing all plants you'll learn something new from growing herbs and if you do enough research, you'll dig up all sorts of interesting history about each variety and what they were used for in the past. What's more the simple sight and scent of herbs do what plants do best, help reduce stresses and worries and revitalise you when you're down. Not only are they good for us but so many varieties of herbs are also great for attracting pollinators. Thyme, lavender, chives, and rosemary will have bees and butterflies flocking to visit. It's a win-win.

So where to begin? Basil, coriander, and parsley are good kitchen staple herbs, which can be sown from seed and grown on your kitchen windowsill. In the warmer months they can go outside if space allows.

As a general rule of thumb, I try to grow as many perennial plants as possible and the same rule applies when growing perennial herbs. These can be grown in pots or in the ground outside all year round and require little fuss. My key players, which work the hardest in the garden and in the kitchen include mint, chives, rosemary, thyme, sage, and lavender. However, grow what you like and experiment.

Picture perfect harvests from
the back garden...

Homegrown and homecooked

We created the recipes in the book at home throughout the various lockdowns, almost an edible diary of the seasons I guess you could say, of what we grew and cooked with from our back garden. I also wanted to illustrate what can be cooked from household staples you can grow yourself. They show what you can take from your own growing space straight into your kitchen. There is nothing more satisfying than cooking with fresh ingredients, except maybe seeing the amazement on a child's face as you pull a wonky carrot out of the earth.

The recipes are also accessible to both children and adults, encouraging experimentation from an early age, but also straightforward enough to ensure children can get involved in every part of the process. We don't sacrifice taste and flavour either. However, I can't guarantee that by growing your own vegetables children will consequently have a healthy appetite for all vegetables for evermore. I wish I could. I really do.

It's also worth noting all the ingredients I suggest you try growing can be grown in pots or containers, to ensure they are accessible to all, including places of education.

The recipes and ingredients are also truly international – while the UK might be the prime focus initially, if it can grow in Glasgow, it can pretty much be grown anywhere!

Before you start, I think it's important to bear in mind that although it can be really tempting once you have the itch to start sowing ALL yours seeds in February and March, leaving you with thousands of seedlings without homes, sowing little and often is key. We call this successional sowing.

It's also okay to hold off to at least March and even April, especially, if like us, you live further north. There is always the possibility of a freak snowstorm and Arctic conditions in May. You just never can be too sure. If you sow little and often through the growing season, you're less likely to have gaps where you have nothing to pick or eat.

Finally, my golden rule for growing your own, which is of paramount importance, is grow what you and those you are growing alongside like to eat.

You don't need a greenhouse to grow your own

Cooking from what you grow yourself makes you look at simple ingredients that you would normally just chuck in your supermarket trolley in a completely different light. A carrot suddenly becomes versatile, to be used in so many ways, while gluts of fruit and veg make you determined not to waste a tiny scrap. As you will soon learn, a lot of love, sweat, and tears go into growing your own. Things are not always straightforward, sometimes there are epic fails, but a huge amount of fun is also to be had.

Potatoes

Potatoes are classified into two camps, 'earlies', which you harvest mid-summer and are known as new potatoes and then there are 'maincrop' potatoes, which are in the ground longer and harvested later, providing a larger crop.

Order seed potatoes from January, which look like normal supermarket potatoes but are certified as being virus free so they will not spread or harbour any disease in your crop. To get a head start, begin chitting your early potatoes in February. This involves placing your seed potatoes in an egg carton with the eye end up in a light, frost-free place such as a porch until you see signs of short green shoots about 3 cm long.

Plant first earlies in late March, second earlies from the beginning to mid-April, and your main crop in late April. They will need lots of peat-free compost, homemade compost, or well-rotted farm manure. I find growing potatoes in containers to be a good use of space and you'll have so much fun raking about when it comes to harvesting them.

How to. Plant in deep containers, begin by filling the container with 15 cm of compost and plant two or three seed potatoes just below this and cover. To protect the developing shoots, earth them up. This means adding more compost until your container is full to the top as the new stems grow. If potatoes are exposed to light when growing they will turn green and become poisonous.

Harvest. Leave your plant to flower and don't be alarmed when the leaves start to shrivel and turn a yellow colour. This is all part of the process. Allow the foliage to die back and then dig for your treasure. Potatoes will keep well, unwashed, in a hessian sack, in a cool dark place. First earlies will be ready to harvest from June (10- 12 weeks after planting) and second earlies will be ready mid-July to early August (10 – 12 weeks). Maincrop potatoes will be ready from late August to October (15 – 20 weeks). Remove the leaves once they turn yellow. Leave the potatoes in the ground for 10 days and then harvest your main crop. Allow them to dry before storing.

Fun facts. Although potatoes are associated with Ireland, they were first cultivated in South America by indigenous communities such as the Incas in the Andes. They were not introduced to Europe until the middle of the 16th century.

Waste not, want not. Wasting food is officially out of fashion. I am calling it. Rescuing food that would have otherwise ended up in landfill is to be encouraged. Despite potatoes being one of our most popular vegetables, almost 800,000 tonnes of potatoes are wasted every year. That's an awful lot of tatties! If you've made too much mash, don't chuck it out, let it cool and freeze in a container or freezer bag. Too many boiled potatoes? Cut into wedges, add a little olive oil and rosemary and roast to make potato wedges. Potatoes are also the backbone to any good frittata, the ultimate fridge raid meal, ideal for using up leftovers in the fridge.

Favourite varieties. 'Red Duke of York' (first early), 'Charlotte' (second early) and 'King Edward' & 'Maris Piper' (maincrop)

Get a head start. Chitting first and second early seed potatoes in an egg carton helps bolster growth.

Digging for treasure. Every child, and adult, will love harvesting potatoes.

1kg potatoes

4 eggs

2 tbsp olive oil

25g unsalted butter

1 whole garlic bulb

One handful of fresh rosemary

Hot sauce. Entirely optional and amount dependent on how fiery your taste buds can handle.

Boiled and bashed tatties

Growing up potatoes made an appearance on our plates most supper times. I detested them. In fact, our dog was frequently fed them under the kitchen table. However, fast forward a decade, or two, and I have a newfound love for the humble spud if it hasn't been boiled to death and it isn't served with mince. Dressed up, they are a welcome guest on any dinner plate, especially this hearty dish.

1. Begin by bringing a big pot of water to the boil and boil your potatoes for 10-12 minutes until tender.

2. Drain the water and using the back of a fork gently bash the potatoes, breaking the skin. This will make them super crispy.

3. Pop the potatoes into a large roasting tray, drizzle over the olive oil, add in the garlic cloves, unpeeled, and rosemary.

4. Roast in a preheated oven at 180C for a good 50 minutes.

5. Shortly before the potatoes are ready, fry four eggs in a little butter. Put the eggs on top of the potatoes and add some hot sauce.

500g potatoes

280g tomatoes

2 tbsp balsamic vinegar

6 garlic cloves

A good drizzle of olive oil

One handful of fresh basil leaves torn up

Potato and tomato salad

It's not to say I don't like boiled potatoes. I do. Slathered in butter or mixed with yoghurt and wild garlic pesto and topped with chopped spring onions they are delicious. However, I cannot get enough of roasted potatoes, especially in the summer when your tomatoes are ripening. This could easily be a main dish or one of many side dishes, probably served with sausages in our house.

1. Preheat the oven to 180C and place the potatoes and garlic cloves unpeeled, on a baking tray. Cover with olive oil. Bake for 50 minutes.

2. After 30 minutes add in the tomatoes, drizzle with a little more olive oil and the balsamic vinegar and cook for the last 20 minutes until the tomatoes begin to sizzle and pop.

3. Finish by covering the dish in fresh basil leaves.

Pumpkins

If I had to choose one fruit to grow on a dessert island, it would be pumpkins. Pumpkins have become a bit of an obsession in our back garden, after visiting Kilduff Farm's culinary patch in the heart of East Lothian in 2019. In fact, if I were to get carried away, which is known to happen from time to time, I think I could fill this entire book with pumpkin recipes. I've held back as much as I could – a difficult challenge, hence a few extra pumpkin recipes.

Nutritious, versatile, and delicious, pumpkins are underrated. Associated with Halloween they're then cast away. I'm here to change that perspective and champion the pumpkin, the gem in autumn's crown. They don't just magically appear on supermarket shelves for a few weeks in October and then vanish into the darkness along with the ghouls and the witches. Harvested in September and October, they can be stored and kept right through into the New Year and beyond.

The kaleidoscope of colours, variety of shapes and mesmerising names are enough to engage anyone. What's more the culinary varieties, which are a far cry from the gigantic, watery, orange carving varieties, taste so good. There's no need to buy sweet potatoes, flown in from far-flung places ever again.

My favourite is the 'Crown Prince' variety. A steely blue-grey colour on the outside and bright orange on the inside. It smells like fresh melon when sliced open and tastes sublime roasted with olive oil and the skin left on. I also love the 'Tractor' variety, which I have dubbed the pudding pumpkin. Perfect for making cakes, muffins and even ice cream as it's very sweet and creamy tasting when puréed.

They are however fussy plants, a bit like small children seated around the kitchen table, and you will need patience. A great quality to nurture, I'm sure you'll agree.

Once they get going, they grow at a monstrous rate and will quickly take over the garden. However, the excitement you get from watching one tiny seed germinate and rapidly growing into a hungry, sprawling plant never disappoints. They also provide a welcome pop of colour in the garden as everything else begins to slowly retreat and retire ahead of winter.

'Crown Prince' pumpkins are our favourite culinary variety.

How to. Begin by sowing seeds indoors in small pots from mid-April. Yoghurt tubs are perfect. Once they've germinated and are established, pot on and then plant outside in June into the ground or into a very large, deep container. They need lots of feeding, lots of water and they really don't like the wind, so keep them in a sheltered spot. You'll discover slugs find them tasty too. Once the fruit begins to grow larger, pop a piece of wood underneath it. Each plant should grow two, maybe three, fruits, so remove any smaller fruits that don't quite seem to be making progress and are turning yellow.

Harvest. Wait until the pumpkin has become hard and sounds hollow when tapped, normally the end of September, start of October. Leave for about a week and cut it leaving a good three inches of the pumpkin stem to prevent rot. This will allow them to be stored for longer if kept in a cool, dark place.

Fun facts. Pumpkins are a fruit and come from the Cucurbitaceae family, otherwise known as the gourd family, along with cucumbers too. They are also an unsung super-food packed with Vitamin A & C, high in potassium and fibre.

Waste not want not. Around 8 million tonnes of pumpkin ends up in landfill every year after Halloween. Not only is that a horrifying figure, it's also a lot of pumpkin pie to have missed out on! What many people still don't realise is that, not only are the seeds and the flesh edible but the skin is too. The skin of both the 'Crown Prince' and 'Kuri' is delicious. Cut into chunks, they make great wedges. The larger varieties are a solid vehicle for spices such as cumin, ginger and chilli in soups – and don't forget the seeds. Simply scoop them out and roast them with cumin and fennel seeds, a little olive oil and honey.

Favourite varieties. 'Crown Prince', 'Tractor' and 'Porcelain Doll'. If tight on space 'Jack Be Little' is a good variety to grow. Pumpkins of all shapes and sizes can also be grown vertically.

Top Tips. Pumpkins may be bright and bold but like us they love company. Sunflowers, nasturtiums, and marigolds make for great companion plants so try growing these nearby to help boost the growth of your pumpkin. They will help attract pollinators and keep away any nasty bugs that may like to feast on your prized pumpkin plant.

1 medium 'Crown Prince' or traditional carving pumpkin

2 white onions

A good knob of butter

1.5 litres good quality vegetable or chicken stock

1 tsp cumin seeds

1 tbsp garam masala

1 tsp ground cinnamon

A handful of pumpkin seeds and calendula petals to serve (optional)

Pumpkin and garam masala soup

Warming and comforting, this pumpkin soup recipe is everything a soup should be. It's basically a hug in a bowl, which will leave you feeling ever so wholesome. Along with the ability to make a solid roast chicken, to be able to cook a pot of soup is something everyone should have up their sleeve. So why not make it a pumpkin soup?

1. Use one half of a medium sized 'Crown Prince' pumpkin. Leave the skin on, remove the seeds and cut into chunks. This helps the pumpkin keep its shape.

2. Drizzle with olive oil and roast in a pre-heated oven at 180C for 40 minutes.

3. Peel and finely dice the onions and fry in butter with the cumin seeds for at least 15 minutes on a low heat. Be careful not to burn the onions.

4. Once the pumpkin has been roasted, remove the skin (you can then snack on it!) and add the pumpkin flesh to the onions.

5. Add the vegetable or chicken stock and bring to the boil.

6. Add the garam masala and cinnamon and leave everything to simmer on a low heat for 20 minutes.

7. Blitz until smooth and serve with a scattering of pumpkin seeds and calendula petals.

Half of one small sized pumpkin, seeds removed & skin left on. We've used the Amoro variety for this recipe. Crown Prince would also work well.

Three or four small/medium sized courgettes.

2 tbsp full fat Greek yoghurt

2 tsp tahini

2 tsp runny honey

A good drizzle of olive oil

One handful of pumpkin seeds and calendula petals (optional)

Courgette and pumpkin salad

This recipe marries the last of the courgettes and the first of the pumpkins. If you are lucky enough to have had a warm summer then you'll have a glut of courgettes, which I never find to be a problem, and you may find yourself harvesting your pumpkins a little earlier than usual. Ideal as a dish on its own served with bread, or it makes for a delicious side dish.

1. Begin by preheating the oven to 180C

2. Chop the pumpkin into similar sized wedges and evenly spread them over a roasting tin. Use two tins if needed. Drizzle olive oil over the top and roast for 35 minutes, turning halfway through.

3. Slice the courgettes into discs and fry in a little olive oil for approximately 5 minutes on each side or until golden brown.

4. Meanwhile make the dressing. Whisk together the yoghurt, tahini and honey.

5. Place the pumpkin and the courgette on a warm plate and spoon the dressing over the roasted vegetables – use as little or as much of the dressing as you fancy. Sprinkle over the pumpkin seeds and calendula petals if using. Serve and eat while warm.

Pumpkin patch kids. Pumpkins have to be our favourite crop grown in our back garden.

Shot by Nick Mailer at
Kilduff Farm in East Lothian

Cake

200g unsalted butter plus extra for greasing

220g light brown sugar

2 eggs

250g grated pumpkin. We've used the 'Red Kuri' variety for this recipe.

Zest of 1 orange (Keep a little bit aside for the icing.)

2 tsp ground ginger

200g self-raising flour

Icing

150g unsalted butter

300g icing sugar

1 tbsp cream cheese

A little extra orange zest

You will also need

1 x 20 cm cake tin

A mixture of brambles, figs, calendula & nasturtium flowers to decorate (optional)

An autumn celebration cake

I first baked this cake for a photoshoot I was styling for Kilduff Farm (pictured left!) and it is now a favourite showstopper as we get wound up in autumn's golden fever. Perfect for a celebration or just for yourself as the days begin to get shorter. Cut a big slice. Pour a mug of tea. Enjoy. We won't tell anyone.

1. Preheat the oven to 170C and grease and line your cake tin.

2. Put the butter, sugar and eggs into an electric mixer and beat until light and fluffy.

3. Fold in the grated pumpkin, orange zest and ground ginger.

4. Next, gently fold in the self-raising flour until combined and then transfer the batter into the cake tin.

5. Cover the cake with foil and bake for 60 minutes. Remove the foil and bake for a further 20 minutes. Test the mixture is cooked by inserting a skewer into the cake and, if ready, it will come out clean. If any wet batter sticks to the skewer, bake for a further 10 minutes and test again.

6. Leave to cool completely before icing. Resist the temptation!

7. To make the icing, beat the butter in a kitchen mixer or use an electric hand whisk until lovely and light. Add in the icing sugar and whisk both ingredients together. Add a tablespoon of full fat cream cheese to the icing to take the edge off the sweetness and stir through the orange zest..

8. Decorate with nasturtiums, blackberries and figs to make an impression – entirely optional!

Half of one small to medium sized pumpkin. 'Crown Prince' is perfect for this recipe.

10 good quality sausages

3 white onions.

2 large red apples

6 garlic cloves unpeeled

4 tbsp olive oil

4 tsp honey

One large handful of blackberries

One handful of pumpkin seeds

Pumpkin and sausage traybake

With three small boys, sausages have long been the star character of mealtimes in our house and who doesn't love a one-pot dinner? They've come to my rescue on many an occasion when faced with a supper time conundrum. This one is not only their favourite but also mine. I know fruit cooked with meat is a bit like Marmite but trust me, this one is a winner. Serve with some good quality bread to mop up the juices.

1. Begin by preheating the oven to 180C.

2. Peel and chop the onions into chunks, and core and chop two large red apples into chunks.

3. Cut one medium pumpkin in half. The 'Crown Prince' variety is again perfect for this recipe. Remove the seeds with a spoon. Use one half and cut into similar sized chunks. Use the other half of the pumpkin for a soup.

4. Add the sausages, the apples, onions, whole garlic cloves and pumpkin to the tray, making sure everything is evenly spaced out and not piled on top of one another. Scatter a handful of pumpkin seeds over the top.

5. Mix the olive oil and honey together in a bowl. Drizzle all over the ingredients. Bake in the oven for 40 – 45 minutes and turn everything halfway through.

6. Ten minutes from the end, add a good handful of blackberries for an extra autumnal blast.

Quarter of a 'Crown Prince' pumpkin

2 medium sized white onions

A knob of butter

A good drizzle of olive oil

2 tsp coriander seeds

2 tsp cumin seeds

2 tsp chilli flakes

4 cloves of garlic, peeled and chopped

A thumb-sized piece of fresh ginger, peeled and chopped

500g red lentils

1 tin chopped tomatoes

1 litre vegetable stock

1 tin full fat coconut milk

Two handfuls of fresh coriander

Pumpkin dahl

Dahl is one of my favourite meals. Thrifty and filling, it's also a great way to introduce children to different spices, so feel free to play around with how much or how little you add. It also freezes well and is a great dish to make if you are looking to make batches of something to stash in the freezer.

1. Take your pumpkin, remove the seeds, chop into equal sized chunks, drizzle with olive oil and roast at 180C for about 30 -35 minutes.

2. Peel, slice & dice the onions and fry in butter with the chopped garlic until golden brown. Patience is key. One should never rush an onion and be sure not to take your eye off the hob.

3. Add the coriander seeds and cumin seeds.

4. Next add the red lentils, the chopped tomatoes, fresh ginger and veg stock.

5. Bring to the boil and cook on a low heat for 25 minutes. Make sure it doesn't stick to the bottom of the pot.

6. Towards the end of cooking time, add the coconut milk and a good handful of fresh coriander.

7. Stir through the roasted pumpkin.

8. Serve with rice and more fresh coriander.

One quarter of a small pumpkin

2 small beetroot

1 small carrot

320g shop-bought puff pastry

6 tsp harissa paste pesto

1 handful pine nuts

2 tbsp olive oil

1 tbsp milk

2 tsp cumin

The autumn veg patch raid tart

Shop-bought puff pastry is something I always have in the fridge and is great when cooking with children. It becomes the solid foundation of a meal in minutes. This tart is not only colourful and inviting, it's also super easy to make. It evolved by accident as I was clearing our veg patch and found one lonesome carrot and some beetroot I had forgotten about, and a chunk of pumpkin left over from the night before. Waste not, want not!

1. Preheat the oven to 180C and set aside a large baking tray.

2. Scrub the carrot and beetroot clean and peel. Chop into evenly sized small chunks and chop the leftover pumpkin into small chunks too. Spread over the baking paper, making sure the veg is not on top of one another and the tray is not overcrowded. Drizzle over the olive oil and the cumin seeds. Roast for 25 minutes.

3. Roll out your puff pastry and using a knife carefully mark out a 2 cm border around the side. Spread the harissa paste pesto out on the inside of the pastry. Add the veg on top and then finish by sprinkling some pine nuts over and brushing the sides of the tart with a little milk using a pastry brush.

4. Bake in the already hot oven at 180C for a further 25 minutes or until the edges of the tart are golden brown.

Makes 1 loaf

For the dough

500g strong white bread flour, plus extra for dusting the tray and work surface

10g salt

1 tsp instant dried yeast

50ml extra virgin olive oil and a little extra for drizzling once baked

For the topping

One quarter of 'Crown Prince' pumpkin or any squash/pumpkin

75g Gorgonzola

1 large handful of fresh rosemary sprigs and sage leaves

Pumpkin & Gorgonzola focaccia

Focaccia is a very forgiving bread to bake, if like me, bread is not your medal-winning speciality in the kitchen. However, it looks impressive. It's also a great vehicle for carrying all sorts of delicious goodness on top and so is quite like a pizza, but a little chunkier and more bread-like. In fact, in some parts of Italy it is called "pizza bianca" (white pizza).

The recipe for the dough is inspired by one of my food heroes, Gill Meller, who not only creates the most sublime dishes but when it comes to flavour and turning the ordinary into something very special, is a master of his art. I draw so much inspiration from his cooking.

I should add that this focaccia should come with a warning. If made, it will not last long. Only one thing for it, best make two.

1. Take a large bowl and into that goes the flour, salt, and yeast. Add the extra virgin olive oil along with 400ml of water. Using your hands, combine it all together to make a ball of wet dough.

2. You can turn the dough onto a floured surface and knead it for a good 10 minutes if you fancy a workout, or you can also use a mixer, with a dough hook, if you prefer. This is my preference. You want the dough to be soft and smooth by the end of the kneading process.

3. Make the dough into a round shape and drop it into the bowl, which should be slightly oiled to stop the dough from sticking. Cover with a tea towel and leave in a warm place for 2 hours. It should double in size during this time.

4. While this is happening, take a quarter of a 'Crown Prince' pumpkin with the skin on and cut into small evenly sized chunks. Place on a baking tray and drizzle the olive oil over the top. Roast in the oven at 180C for 30 minutes or until soft.

5. Preheat the oven to 200C. Put a little flour on a small baking tray and turn the dough out onto the tray, making sure it is right up to the edges of the tray. Next, press the pumpkin into the dough along with the Gorgonzola, the sage and rosemary. Cover and leave for a further 45 minutes.

6. Before putting the dough into the oven, drizzle with olive oil and bake for 40 minutes. The bread should be cooked through and golden in colour.

While I am all for cooking with pumpkins, I do also love creating alternative 'works of art' from them. They make for super stylish alternatives to a vase. Simply take the top off the pumpkin, scoop out the seeds and any of the flesh you can without damaging the skin.

You can paint the outside of the pumpkin using tester pots you might have hidden away or leave it be if you prefer. Fill a jam jar with water and place inside the pumpkin. Finally, all that is left to be done is to pick some flowers from your garden or forage some greenery from your local wooded area and there you have it, a fun and colourful home-grown and homemade table centrepiece. Really easy, yet effective.

Peas

I have become reliant on a bag of frozen peas, stashed away at the back of the freezer. The saviour of many a dinner-time meal in need of 'greening up'. However, nothing compares to the taste of home-grown peas. Plus, they don't take up too much space, can be grown in pots and look good too as they soar up into the sky. Children love picking and shelling them, and some might even enjoy eating them! We can but hope.

How to. For sweet-tasting peas, choose a sunny spot in the garden. Improve your soil by adding peat-free compost and well-rotted farm manure. From early spring, dig a wide trench roughly 4 cm deep and water the trench before sowing. This helps stimulate quick germination. Sow the seeds 5 cm apart and keep rows 15 cm apart.

Once your pea seedlings are established, create tepees from canes or sticks so the peas have something to climb up.

If you want to make sure you have a continuous supply of peas throughout the summer, sow more seeds every 10-14 days if space allows. Remember to water well after sowing.

Harvest. Peas will be ready to harvest round about 12 to 15 weeks after sowing once the pods look as though they have swollen with the peas inside them. To make sure you get lots, pick every day, just like sweet peas. This way, the plant will be encouraged to produce more and more peas for you to enjoy.

Top Tip. Water once a week once the peas start to flower. To prevent the pea plant from drying out when it is very warm, add a layer of mulch around the base of the plant. This will lock in moisture and strengthen the growth of the plant.

Fun Fact. Did you know most frozen peas you find in the freezer section of the supermarket are frozen within two-and-a-half hours of being picked? This way, all the nutrients are locked into each pea so we can enjoy the benefits.

The very first peas were frozen by the American inventor and entrepreneur Clarence Birdseye who in the 1920's and 30's developed frozen food technology, which would preserve foods for longer.

Waste not, want not. If you find yourself in the fortunate position of producing a huge amount of peas, more than you could happily gobble, in the garden, fear not. Once you've shelled them, you can freeze them in bags or in tubs for a taste of garden-fresh peas all year long – great for adding to soup or risotto straight from frozen.

Favourite variety. 'Avola' & 'Canoe'.

I prefer peas as a side dish dressed up with a little olive oil and mint leaves. However, if you do grow them and stash them in your freezer, they make for a quick and easy pea and roasted garlic soup, straight from frozen into a hot vegetable stock. You can also add in some lettuce (yes, really) and some courgettes, as well as a white onion, mint leaves, and blitz until smooth. In our house, we call this dinosaur soup. It's a fresh summery soup. You can also add the frozen peas to a risotto or even a frittata. Peas, rice, and mint sauce is another winner.

Rhubarb

No growing area is complete without at least one trusty rhubarb crown growing in a corner. It's super easy to grow and every year you will have delicious stalks to create crumbles, cakes, and cordials.

How to. Plant rhubarb crowns between September and October or between April and May in an open sunny or partially shaded area in rich, fertile ground. It can also be grown in a container. If planting more than one in the ground, ensure the crowns are planted at least 90 cm apart from each other as they will spread.

You can also force rhubarb in late winter by covering the crowns to prevent light from getting in. This encourages the plant to grow earlier than normal. It is, however, recommended you wait until your rhubarb plant is well- established before you attempt to force it. Stems will be shorter and sweeter and will be ready to pick from late winter, early spring.

Harvest. Don't harvest your rhubarb in the first year. The following year, you can pick a few stems and they should be ready from spring onwards. You shouldn't need a knife. Pull and twist the stem and in turn this will stimulate more growth.

Top tip. Do not eat the leaves. Rhubarb leaves are very poisonous so remove and add them to your garden compost pile.

Fun fact. Rhubarb is not a fruit but a vegetable. Just don't tell the kids!

The UK's largest rhubarb collection is in the Walled Kitchen Garden at Clumber Park. It's home to more than 130 varieties of rhubarb and is the second largest collection in the world.

Waste not, want not. If you are faced with a glut and can't give enough of your rhubarb away, you can cut it into chunks and freeze it for when you fancy an impromptu rhubarb crumble in November.

Favourite varieties. 'Strawberry', 'Victoria' & 'Timperley Early'.

500g chopped rhubarb

100g unsalted butter

200g ginger biscuits

3 pieces of stem ginger chopped and diced

2 tsp stem ginger syrup

150g caster sugar

500g soft full fat cream cheese

100g Greek full fat yoghurt

Rhubarb cheesecake

This is a summer pudding not to be sniffed at and again a cheesecake is a great pudding to nail early on in life. What's more, what child will not enjoy bashing the biscuits in a bag with a rolling pin?!

1. Chop the rhubarb into chunks and place on a roasting tray and sprinkle with sugar and bake in the oven at 170 C for about 15 minutes. Reserve a third for the top and pour the rest in a food blender with the cream cheese filling.

2. While the rhubarb is baking bash the ginger biscuits in a bag with a rolling pin. Then gently melt the butter in a pan and stir in the biscuit crumb mixture. Take off the heat and stir in three pieces of chopped stem ginger.

3. Press the biscuit mixture into a 30 cm loose bottom cake tin and set aside.

4. In a glass bowl gently fold together the cream cheese and yoghurt and stir in the rhubarb purée. Spoon the mixture on top of the biscuit base and add the chopped rhubarb you reserved earlier, on top. Leave in the fridge for four to six hours before serving.

400g strawberries

4 stalks of rhubarb

2 tbsp light brown soft sugar

Roasted rhubarb and strawberries

The tartness of the rhubarb and the sweetness of the strawberries really work well together when you combine the two. Also if you have too many strawberries and they are beginning to go a little soft and mushy this is a great dish to try to prevent any food waste. It also makes for a really tasty pudding idea, served with yoghurt, honey and maybe even some toasted almond flakes if you really want to push the boat out.

1. Preheat the oven to 180C.

2. Chop the rhubarb into similar sized chunks and place on a large baking tray. Cut the strawberries into half and place over the rhubarb and then sprinkle the sugar over the top.

3. Place in the oven for 10-12 minutes, or until nice and soft.

300g rhubarb chopped into chunks

145g frozen raspberries

195g ground almonds

200g unsalted butter

150g light brown sugar

4 medium sized free-range eggs

A small handful of whole almonds chopped into pieces.

Rhubarb and raspberry pudding

If all the stars align when you are growing fruit and vegetables, you can end up with some great combinations to cook with, like rhubarb and raspberries. Or if they don't, frozen raspberries are fine to use and are in fact a kitchen staple in our house.

1. Preheat the oven to 180C and layer the chopped rhubarb and frozen raspberries into a 30 cm cake tin.

2. Using a food mixer, combine the sugar and the butter until light and fluffy, mix in the ground almonds and the eggs and combine everything together.

3. Pour the cake mixture on top of the rhubarb and raspberries and sprinkle a handful of the chopped almond chunks on top.

4. Bake in the oven for 40-50 minutes or until golden brown and cooked through.

Tomatoes

Our middle child is, in his own words, 'The Tomato King'. He can't get enough of them. I can't blame him. Home-grown tomatoes are sublime and the seasonal star of any summer garden. You'll never eat another supermarket tomato in December again. The variety of colours, shapes, and sizes to choose from is enough to make you want to grow your own. You'll just have to hope the dreaded curse, which is blight, bypasses your crop.

While Reuben may be the champion eater of tomatoes, my grandmother Margaret is the champion grower. Her tomatoes are epic and will be long etched on my memory and my taste buds. I have fond memories of stepping into her greenhouse. I can smell the scent and taste of the sweet flavour today, as I type this during winter, transporting me back to the dizzy heights of summer. When I grow up, I want to be a tomato grower just like her.

How to. Begin by sowing and growing seeds in small pots on the windowsill from February through to April. They will taste so much better if grown in full sun and in rich peat-free compost. Keep potting them on as they grow bigger and need a larger pot, keeping them on your warm windowsill.

After the last frost has passed, choose a sunny sheltered spot and plant one plant into a large container or a grow bag and keep well-watered. You can also grow them in a greenhouse if you are lucky enough to have one or keep them inside! Again, keep them well watered. If you don't water them regularly, this will cause blossom end rot, a result of poor calcium uptake due to irregular watering. So, if you go away on holiday, be sure to get a good friend or neighbour to keep your plants well hydrated.

Harvest. The tomatoes will ripen on the plant, making them even sweeter. They taste like heaven when freshly picked and still warm from the heat of the sun, although if you eat them all, this may spoil plans for supper.

Towards the end of the season, the leaves may begin to look a little tired. Remove them to let the last of the summer light in, helping the last few remaining tomatoes to ripen.

Top tips. If you are growing a cordon variety of tomatoes, these will need to be pinched out. This means removing any side shoots. They'll also need to be staked to help strengthen growth. You don't have to do either if you are growing a bushy variety – great for beginners. These can also be grown in hanging baskets.

Once flowers appear on your plant, it's a good idea to feed them a weekly liquid tomato feed.

Don't store your tomatoes in the fridge. They taste so much better kept at room temperature.

Planting basil alongside tomatoes helps them grow stronger and boosts their flavour. French marigolds are also a great companion plant for tomatoes. The strong odour will help keep greenfly and blackfly at bay.

Fun facts. Tomatoes are a fruit, and they are not just red but come in a rainbow of different colours, including orange, yellow, purple and even black.

Tomatoes were first introduced into Europe in the 16th century and, due to their appearance, they were known as 'golden apples' as they were small and golden.

Waste not, want not. If you have any tomatoes left over, which is hard to imagine I know, make your own tomato sauce to freeze for pasta or a pizza base. Fry a couple of medium-sized onions with three or four cloves of garlic thinly sliced and add fresh basil and, of course, tomatoes. Use a blender to create a smooth consistency before freezing in containers or bags.

Favourite varieties. 'Gardeners Delight', good for growing outdoors & 'Tumbling Tom Red', good for baskets and pots. 'Money Maker' and 'Ailsa Craig' are also reliable favourites to grow.

800g tomatoes

2 medium white onions, peeled and diced

4 garlic cloves, peeled and chopped

2 tsp cumin seeds

2 tsp coriander seeds

300g soft light brown sugar

250ml white wine vinegar

Tomato jam

Grown a glut of tomatoes some of which are still green and showing no sign of ripening? Welcome to my world. You and I can be friends. This recipe is for you and is a perfect gifting opportunity. However, you won't be judged if you decide to just eat it with cheese and biscuits. Either option is fine and feel free to double the quantities if the glut is really large.

1. Toast the cumin and coriander seeds on a low heat for about 1 minute and then, using a pestle and mortar give them a bash.

2. Using a large soup pot, add in the chopped onion with 30g of butter and gently fry the onions until they are golden brown and sweet.

3. Next add in the garlic along with the spices, the tomatoes, sugar, and the vinegar.

4. Bring to the boil and then gently cook on a low heat, stirring occasionally until you have created a jam-like consistency.

5. Once cooled, divide your tomato jam into sterilised jam jars and keep in the fridge.

Courgettes

The courgette is the one vegetable I grow in pots year after year. They are also very easy to grow and will keep producing throughout the summer providing you with a delicious crop for soups, cakes, and salads. As they are so prolific you can be sure you'll have enough not only for yourselves but also for friends and neighbours too, even if you grow only two or three plants.

How to. Sow two seeds on their sides in small pots indoors. This prevents the seed from rotting. Cover with compost, water, and grow on your windowsill throughout April or May. When seedlings appear, remove the stronger one and pot it up into a bigger pot and continue to grow on inside. From the end of May into June, you can plant out your young plants into large containers filled with peat-free compost and well- rotted farm manure, if you can get it. Give them a weekly liquid tomato feed and keep them well-watered.

Harvest. Your courgettes should be ready from July right through until September and sometimes even October. Once they are about 10 cm in length, they are ripe for picking. Don't let them get any bigger. They won't taste as good and the more you pick the more, you'll be able to harvest for longer. You can harvest using a knife.

Top tips. Keep courgette plants constantly moist to ensure you get the best from your summer crop. Water regularly and apply a mulch around the base of the plant to lock in moisture.

If you see signs of mildew, which looks like a white powdery coating on the leaves of your courgette plant, remove the affected leaves.

To help bolster the growth of your courgettes, grow nasturtiums and marigolds alongside them. You'll enjoy a burst of colour, and the flowers will help keep pests away. Borage also makes for a great companion. It's beautiful blooms will attract bees, which will pollinate the flowers of the courgette plant.

Fun facts. The flower of the courgette plant is edible and is recognised as a delicacy. It can be stuffed with cheese, fried, and eaten.

Waste not, want not. Courgettes appear in the blink of an eye at the height of summer. Turn your back on them for a day or two and you will return to find marrows. Grated courgette can be frozen in a container with no need to blanch. Remember the skin is the tastiest part, so there's no need to peel. It can also be cut into strips using a vegetable peeler for salads.

If you really do have too many, then always remember to put any excess courgettes into your garden compost, so they can go back into the ground eventually or set up an honesty box at your front door and share the love.

Favourite varieties. 'Romanesco' & 'Soleil'.

3 small courgettes sliced

2 cups of peas, cooked

3 or 4 handfuls salad leaves

For the dressing

2 tbsp olive oil

4 tbsp natural yoghurt

2 tsp runny honey

One handful of sunflower and
pumpkin seeds to finish.

Courgette salad

All three of the starring ingredients in this salad can
be grown at home. Satisfying, rewarding and most
importantly tasty. The key is to fry the courgette slices on
each side for a least four or five minutes on a low heat
until they are a golden-brown colour and not too wet.

As ever don't worry too much about quantities if you don't
have enough of one ingredient or you have too much of
another. Play around and experiment.

1. Add the sliced courgettes into a large, hot frying pan
with a little olive oil and gently fry on a low heat for four
to five minutes. You may have to cook the courgettes in
batches depending on the size of your frying pan.

2. To cook the peas, whether fresh or frozen, simply cover
in boiling water and then drain off the water.

3. To build the salad, use the salad leaves to make the base,
then top with the cooked courgettes, add the peas and then
cover with the yoghurt honey dressing.

4. Finish by topping with sunflower and pumpkin seeds

1 medium sized courgette, grated

50g desiccated coconut

Juice of 1 lime

75g unsalted butter, gently melted in the microwave

300g self-raising flour

1/2 tsp baking powder

100g caster sugar

2 eggs

For the icing

2 tbsp of icing sugar and the juice of another lime, mixed to make a smooth, runny icing. Play around with the quantities of juice and icing sugar to get a consistency you like.

Courgette and coconut muffins

I'm pretty sure at least a couple of these count towards one of your five a day. Baking with vegetables is a great way to show children how versatile different ingredients can be and they don't have to be just boiled and served on the side of their dinner plate.

1. Preheat the oven to 170C and line a muffin tray with 12 cases and lightly oil if not using silicon cases.

2. In a bowl, mix the caster sugar and the melted butter. Sift in the flour, add in the baking powder, and combine all the ingredients together.

3. Next add in both eggs and the grated courgette as well as the desiccated coconut. Finish by squeezing in the juice of one lime and mix together.

4. Divide the cake mixture between each of the 12 cases and bake in the oven for around 25 minutes or until golden brown.

5. Leave to cool and then drizzle over the lime icing.

Strawberries

Is there any other fruit that signals the start of summer more than the strawberry? It is the epitome of the British summer. What's more, like so many other home-grown fruits, strawberries taste so much better when you grow them yourself and are significantly cheaper than those found on the supermarket shelves. Space needn't be an issue if you are keen to grow strawberries, as they work well grown in pots, hanging baskets and window boxes. The only downside of growing strawberries with children is that if you turn your back for just a moment, few strawberries will make it back to the kitchen.

How to. Buy strawberry plants from garden centres or order online in spring. Plant out in a sunny sheltered spot in peat-free compost and well-rotted farm manure. Ensure they are planted 30 – 45 cm apart and that rows are 75 cm apart. Keep them well watered. If growing in a pot make sure it's at least 15 cm wide and grow one plant per pot of this size.

A weekly liquid tomato feed will help promote healthy growth too.

Harvest. From June through to September you should get signs of fruit, depending on if you grow early, main crop or later varieties. Wait until berries are completely red before picking. Eat as soon as they are picked. They'll keep for a few days in the fridge – if they ever get there.

Top tip. Strawberry plants will fruit for at least four years. After this, they'll begin to run out of puff. However, you won't have to buy new plants as they are easy to propagate from runners each year. You'll probably even have enough to give some away to friends and family too. Propagating strawberries is relatively straightforward and a great way to educate children about growing your own.

Begin propagation in early autumn and choose a healthy runner which has already produced one or more leaves. Remove any stems emerging from the new leaves, while keeping it still attached to the parent plant. Fill pots with peat- free compost and place the strawberry runner on the surface and hold it in place with a peg. Keeping the compost moist, wait until the new plant has developed strong roots and then using a pair of scissors snip it away from its parent plant. It can then be replanted into the ground or into a bigger pot.

Mint, dill, sage, and coriander make good companions for strawberries. Just remember if you do decide to grow mint, grow it in its own pot to prevent it from taking over the garden.

Fun facts. Each strawberry contains around 200 seeds!

It's estimated that around 38.4 tonnes of strawberries are eaten by tennis fans at Wimbledon.

Waste not, want not. Mushy strawberries can be turned into a super easy milkshake. Just add milk, some vanilla essence or honey and blitz.

Favourite varieties. 'Cambridge Favourite' and 'Florence'.

Free new plants. Propagating new strawberries from runners is an easy way to replenish your strawberry stocks.

Strawberries, elderflower, and mint

This really isn't a recipe but more an assembly of ingredients combined to make a refreshing dessert or snack, using fresh summer strawberries along with some homemade elderflower cordial.

Take 400g of strawberries, chopped in half. Mix in a small handful of freshly picked mint leaves and stir in 4 tbsp of elderflower cordial. Cover and leave for at least an hour.

Serve with full fat Greek yoghurt and a drizzle of honey.

Base

300g of any sweet biscuits (digestive, rich tea or ginger nut biscuit)

100g unsalted butter

The chocolate mousse

200g dark chocolate solids broken into pieces.

120ml warm water

3 eggs separated

40g golden caster sugar

One small handful of fresh mint leaves

One small handful of strawberries, halved.

Strawberry and chocolate mint cake

I can't take the credit for this. This is in fact the work of my husband Geoff. A man of many talents with a healthy appetite for food. I can also assure you there will not be a slice of this cake left after you serve it. It combines a biscuit base with a chocolate mousse topping, adapted from Delia Smith, Geoff's guiding cookery light, and will finish you off after one good helping. One of Geoff's trademarks.

1. To make the base, blitz the biscuits and the butter in a food processor and press into a pie tin. Aim for a thickness of 2 cm.

2. Place the chocolate and the warm water in a heatproof glass bowl, sit it over a saucepan of barely simmering water, making sure the bowl doesn't touch the water.

3. Keep the heat at a low level and allow the chocolate to melt slowly. Remove the chocolate from the heat and stir until it's smooth and glossy. Let it cool for 2-3 minutes before stirring in the egg yolks. Then give it another good mix.

4. In a clean bowl, whisk the egg whites to the soft-peak stage, then whisk in the sugar, a little at a time. Whisk again until the whites are glossy.

5. Next fold a tablespoon of the egg whites into the chocolate mixture to loosen it, and then fold in the rest. You need to have patience here.

6. Pour the mousse onto the biscuit base and leave it to chill for 2 hours.

7. Before serving add mint leaves and halved strawberries for the finishing touch.

Beetroot

Beetroot is another super easy crop to grow in the garden and the blood red roots, or pink or orange for that matter, are so satisfying to slice into, leaving fingers and hands-stained pink for good measure. It's a versatile ingredient in the kitchen. Think beyond the jars of pickled beetroot. Try it roasted with olive oil and cumin or blitzed into a vibrant hummus. My favourite, however, is when it's baked into a deliciously rich dark chocolate cake. You would never know there was a vegetable hidden within each slice. Part of your five a day for sure.

How to. Beetroot seeds can be sown directly outdoors into the ground from April until June. I use a pencil to make a shallow drill about 1 cm deep and sow the seeds 10 cm apart. If sowing multiple rows, make sure there's about 30 cm between each row. They also like fertile, moist, and sunny conditions and will do just fine in pots too, just make sure they are good and deep.

To ensure you have beetroot from June until Christmas, sow seeds regularly every three to four weeks.

Keep weeds at bay and thin out the weaker seedlings so the stronger ones can thrive. Seedlings should be at least 6 cm apart for optimal growing conditions.

Harvest. You will notice your beetroot is ready to be harvested when the top of the root is bulging through the surface of the soil. The root should be about the size of a tennis or a cricket ball and feel quite tender. Don't pick them any smaller as you'll waste perfectly good beetroot for later.

Waste not, want not. Did you know that you can eat the leaves of beetroot? They are mild and sweet and can be used in salads. Also think twice before you chuck your peelings into the garden compost. These are edible too. Give them a scrub to remove the soil and toss them on to a baking tray with some olive oil, salt and pepper or mix it up with spices and herbs. Try adding rosemary, chilli flakes or cumin for an alternative tasty snack option in the shape of beetroot crisps.

Top tips. There are lots of companion plants that will get along just fine with beetroot in your garden. These include broccoli, brussel sprouts and onions to name but a few.

Fun facts. In the past, beetroot was used as a mouth freshener, to get rid of the smell of garlic, and, in the 19th century, women used beetroot to dye their hair.

Favourite varieties. 'Boltardy' and 'Burpees Golden'.

Beetroot hummus

If there was ever a dish that would turn heads then it would be this beetroot hummus. The vibrancy of the pink is enough to make anyone dive straight in with a slice of bread.

It's also a really great dish to illustrate that all important plot to plate message when you are growing and gardening with children.

Pull two medium sized beetroot out of the ground, chop off the leafy tops and shake off the excess soil. Peel and chop into quarters before cooking in a pan of boiling water until tender. Put the cooked beetroot into a food blender along with a 400g tin of chickpeas drained, 1 tsp of ground cumin, the juice of 2 limes, 2 cloves of garlic, plus 1/2 tsp of salt.

Blitz until smooth and serve with toasted cumin seeds and pine nuts on top or even some fresh mint leaves. If the consistency is too thick, you can add a little water to thin it out.

200g unsalted butter, plus a little extra for greasing the inside of the cake tin.

250g cooked and peeled beetroot, which is roughly about two small beetroots.

100g dark chocolate (70% cocoa solids)

Zest and juice of one large orange

175g self-raising flour

1 heaped tsp baking powder

30g cocoa powder

3 eggs

180g golden caster sugar

Chocolate orange beetroot cake

1. Preheat the oven to 180C and grease a 20 cm/8 in cake tin with a little butter.

2. In a food processor blend the beetroot.

3. Melt the chocolate in a bowl, using the microwave.

4. Remove from the microwave and add the butter to the warm chocolate and allow it to soften.

5. In another bowl sift the flour, baking powder and cocoa together.

6. Add the eggs and the beetroot into the chocolate and fold everything together.

7. Next add the sugar into the flour mixture and then stir in the chocolate mixture until all the ingredients are combined, along with the juice and zest of the orange. You can also use a food mixture to fold everything together for a nice consistency.

8. Pour the batter into the prepared tin and bake for 45-50 minutes, or until a skewer inserted into the cake comes out clean.

9. Allow to cool in the tin and then finish with a dusting of icing sugar.

Carrots

Just like people, carrots come in all shapes and sizes. This is reason enough to grow them, especially when gardening with children. Who doesn't love a wonky carrot, perfectly imperfect? I'm a big champion of wonky veg. We've all become just a little too obsessed with a very clinical and sterile picture of what our food should look like. I'm in the perfectly imperfect camp. It might look a bit dodgy, but it will taste just as good, if not even better when pulled from the ground. The only thing to watch out for when growing carrots is you need to have eyes on the back of your head. My children have a habit of pulling carrots out of the ground before they are ready. Mr McGregor certainly would not be very chuffed.

How to. Carrots prefer growing in soil that is light, loose, and well-drained and some added manure or compost is always a good idea. If you're sowing directly into the ground, be sure to break up big clumps of soil. Carrots are ideal for growing in containers because you can control exactly what type of soil you use.

Using a pencil, make a shallow trench about 1 cm deep and sow your carrot seeds about 5-8 cm apart, from March through to June. The beauty of growing your own carrots is that you're not limited to just long orange carrots. You can sow a wide range of different varieties and colours, which you won't find in the supermarket.

Harvest. Your carrots should be ready from around 10 – 14 weeks after you sow them. Make sure the soil is moist before you pull them out. If not, you run the risk of being left with just the green top and the carrot will still be beneath the soil.

Top tips. To avoid carrot fly, which will destroy your crop, avoid thinning out your carrots. As soon as you start to thin out and crush the leaves of the carrots you will attract this notorious pest. The more common preventative is to cover them or surround with a barrier as the carrot fly travels at a set height from the ground.

Carrots are a great crop to grow in containers, just make sure that your container is deep.

The best companion plants to plant alongside carrots, include chives and onions, which will deter carrot fly. Peas and beans will help improve the soil.

Fun facts. One teaspoon can hold up to 2000 carrot seeds!

We often get told to eat our carrots because they will help us to see in the dark. This idea came about in World War II. The air ministry wanted to prevent the Germans from discovering Britain was using radar to intercept bombers on night raids. The British therefore issued a press release stating British pilots had exceptional night vision due to the large number of carrots they were eating!

Waste not, want not. Did you know the entire carrot is edible. Even the foliage. In fact, the green top of the carrot can be used to make carrot top pesto. Blitz a big bunch with lemon, garlic, pine nuts and cheese.

Favourite varieties; 'Early Nantes 5', 'Purple Sun' and 'Autumn King 2'.

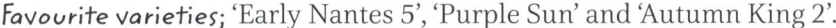

2 carrots peeled and chopped.

A good knob of butter

1 small butternut squash, chopped into chunks, skin left on

2 small white onions peeled and diced.

1 cup red lentils

3 pints vegetable stock

2 tsp cumin seeds

2 tsp coriander seeds

Toasted pine nuts and desiccated coconut to serve or any other seeds and nuts (optional)

Carrot and butternut squash soup

Carrot soup was a good healthy staple for lunch when growing up with lentils added to help bulk it out. I've added butternut squash to this recipe to make it go further and added toasted nuts and desiccated coconut on top to give it a little extra interest, as well as texture and taste.

1. Begin by slowly cooking the diced onion in about 30g of butter on a low heat. Never ever rush an onion. You want it to be golden brown and sweet to taste.

2. While the onion is cooking grind up the cumin and coriander seeds using a mortar and pestle.

3. Next add in the red lentils, chopped carrots and butternut squash, stir through the cumin and coriander seeds.

4. Pour in the vegetable stock and bring to the boil.

5. Simmer on a low heat for about 20 minutes, or until the vegetables are tender. Blitz until smooth using a handheld blender. Season with salt and pepper and add seeds and nuts if you want to.

20g butter, melted.

125g ground almonds

125g grated carrots. About two small carrots.

85g caster sugar

2 eggs

2 tbsp self-raising flour

The zest of 1/2 a large orange

2 tsp ground cinnamon

Carrot cake

Carrot cake is a classic and the ability to bake a good solid carrot cake is a must-have in the armoury of every baker. I would go as far as saying it's up there with an ability to make a good pot of soup, a crumble, and a roast dinner. Four staples to master early on in life.

1. Begin by preheating the oven to 180C.

2. Melt the butter and, using a pastry brush, grease the inside of a loaf tin.

3. In a mixing bowl, mix together the grated carrot, the sugar, the ground almond and the two eggs.

4. Fold in the flour along with the orange zest and cinnamon.

5. Pour the cake mixture into the loaf tin and bake for 40 minutes.

Look How they've Grown

Apples

The best time to plant a tree was 20 years ago. The second-best time is now. Planting one or two trees is something more of us should do both at home and in our communities and schools if space allows. It's a gift for the future, which will keep on giving and will be so beneficial to our natural world. Whether it's an apple, pear, or plum tree, having a fruit tree is a privilege. We planted two the month before the first lockdown in 2020, not realising what was just around the corner. With hindsight, perhaps the trees were a sign that brighter and better times would come again with time. There are varieties and sizes to suit everyone, from hybrid dwarf varieties, which will grow happily in containers, to larger heritage varieties. What's more, adding one or two to a garden is great for wildlife and for attracting pollinators.

How to. Before you start digging a hole, assess how much space you have. When choosing a tree, check to see how big it will grow and how much space it will need. Also choose a type of fruit you really enjoy eating and cooking with.

A sunny sheltered spot is good and it's best to plant fruit trees between November and March as bare roots, which means they are dormant and not flowering or fruiting so won't go into a state of shock. They are also cheaper.

Dig a large hole, ensuring plenty of room for root growth, and add in some peat-free compost and well- rotted manure. Before planting your tree, hammer in a stake for support. Plant the tree so the trunk is level with the ground and back fill the soil in and around the tree. Tie the stake to the tree with a loose tie to allow for growth and give your new tree a good water. Keep watering to ensure the young roots develop well and get established, particularly during a dry spell. You will have to wait a while for the fruits of your labour, but it will be worth it and so rewarding.

Harvest. Apples should be ready to pick between late August and October, but this will depend on what variety of apple you are growing. Apples are generally ripe for picking when you can easily lift and twist them off. While its likely you will be able to eat and cook with them quickly after picking, you can store some varieties in a cool, dark place for a few months. It's worth checking when you buy your tree.

Waste not, want not. Even windfall apples, apples which have fallen off trees, can be eaten despite being bruised and blemished. Peeled, cored and chopped they are perfect for chutney and jelly or even juice. I love to make batches of stewed apple sauce, which freezes well. Simply core, peel and chop the apples, add to a pan with a splash of apple juice and 2 tsp of ground cinnamon and cover with a lid. Gently cook until the apple softens. If you are lucky enough to have a well-established fruit tree, why not leave some apples for neighbours to help themselves? Friendships are made and recipes shared.

Top tip. Most apple trees need pollinators to help them flower and fruit so plant them alongside other fruit trees and in an area that is rich in other bee- friendly flowers. Nasturtiums, lavender, and rosemary are just a few good companion suggestions, which will attract pollinators, deter pests, and help enrich the soil.

Fun facts. There are thousands of varieties of apples grown around the world so it is worthwhile growing your own as you could grow a variety you wouldn't be able to buy readily in the supermarket.

We've all heard the saying "An *apple a day keeps the doctor away"* and apples are a healthy snack as each apple contains 5g of fibre and antioxidants, most of which is in the skin of the apple.

175g unsalted butter, softened.

150g caster sugar

3 eggs

250g self – raising flour

2 tsp ground cinnamon

50ml milk

2 large cooking apples, peeled, cored, and thinly sliced.

A little brown sugar to sprinkle on top of the cake before baking.

Spiced apple cake

Apples have many uses, but a spiced apple cake must be one of my favourite recipes. This is a simple yet delicious finisher to any supper and could be served warm with a dollop of custard on top.

1. Preheat the oven to 160C and grease and line a 30 cm cake tin.

2. Cream together the butter and caster sugar in a food mixer until light and fluffy.

3. Beat in the eggs one at a time, followed by the flour and cinnamon. Slowly add the milk and gently combine.

4. Place half the batter into the prepared cake tin, followed by a layer of apple slices. Gently spread the remaining batter on top and finish with another layer of apple slices and a sprinkling of brown sugar.

5. Bake in the oven for 40-45 minutes or until well-risen and golden brown in colour. Use a skewer to test if it is cooked in the middle. If it comes out clean it is ready. If not bake for a little longer.

6 small apples peeled, cored and chopped.

200g blackberries

2 tbsp soft brown sugar and a little extra for the top.

130g caster sugar

130g butter cut into cubes.

175g plain flour

100g oats

One handful of sunflower seeds.

Apple and blackberry crumble

It has been said that despite being full up after my main meal, I always had room for crumble. In fact, it has been thought I may have a separate tank reserved just for crumble. Once you've mastered the art of the crumble topping, another excellent skill set to harness early on in life, you can go wild with fruit combinations. However, a simple apple crumble will win me over, always.

1. Preheat the oven to 170C and core and chop your apples into medium chunks. Add them to your baking dish, sprinkle the brown sugar on top and add the blackberries.

2. For the crumble topping, get a large bowl and, using your hands rub the butter, the flour, and the caster sugar together until you get a fine crumb. Mix in the oats and the sunflower seeds, using your hands again.

4. Add the crumble mixture to the top of the fruit and add an extra sprinkle of brown sugar on top.

5. Bake in the oven for around 60 minutes.

FORAGING

Nature's supermarket...

Not only does spring signal new growth and hope, but it's also a sign that Mother Nature's larder is about to open for business, providing an exciting world of free, delicious edibles. Around about March time, our walks in the woods and in the nearby countryside get a whole lot tastier.

Foraging with children is basically an edible treasure hunt, giving new purpose to a walk in the great outdoors, allowing them to connect with nature in a new way. It educates them about the plants and leaves surrounding them, providing a sense of control in a world that can sometimes seem intimidating. Foraging also allows children and adults alike to be more mindful of each season and live more in the moment.

It is something to be enjoyed by the whole family but remember one should always err on the side of caution when foraging. If you are unsure what something is, as a rule of thumb, do not pick it. I have listed three of the most common and easily identifiable plants to forage, which are also very tasty and easy to cook with.

Please, do remember when browsing the shelves of nature's supermarket to pick only what you are going to use from areas of plenty. Leave some for other foragers as well as the wildlife and avoid foraging from busy roads.

Wild Garlic

Found in Parks by Rivers in Woodland

Loves damp shady areas

In season March till June

Smells like garlic

Leaves and flowers are edible

Be careful where you pick and not too much in the 1 spot

Also called BEAR's garlic

stay Wild

Wild garlic

If you go down to the woods from March until early May, you'll be pleasantly surprised by an abundance of wild garlic. You will find great swathes of green carpet along riverbanks and moist woodland. It is prolific and more than likely you will recognise the strong garlic smell before you set eyes on the glorious and delicious green leaves.

Wild garlic not only signals the start of spring but is a great place to start if you are new to foraging and is so much fun with children in tow. You could describe it as the gatekeeper to a lifetime interest in foraging, which will grow as your curiosity expands. The young leaves are best picked throughout March, to use in soup, pesto, breads, or even tomato sauces. From April through to June small white flowers will begin to appear. These are edible too and can be used in salads. Pop a whole one in your mouth and you will be guaranteed a strong garlicky kick!

Fun fact. Closely related to the onion family, it's believed wild garlic is much loved by Brown Bears in Europe, hence why it is also known as Bear's Garlic.

Waste not, want not. Wild Garlic freezes well so if you don't manage to use all that you forage within a couple of days, simply rinse it and store in freezer bags in your freezer. This will allow you to enjoy a taste of spring throughout the year.

500g self-raising flour

2 tsp baking powder

200g butter

250g cheddar cheese, grated.

200ml milk & a little extra to brush over the top of the scones before they are baked.

2 handfuls of wild garlic leaves chopped into pieces.

Wild garlic scones

I have wild fantasies of just casually whipping up a batch of warm scones, which are ready just moments before the doorbell rings and friends come to visit or just as the children come home from school, on the cusp of a 'han-gry' meltdown. If you know, you know!

The reality is that this doesn't happen but when wild garlic is in season, I do make a concentrated effort to make these scones. Great on their own or served with soup.

1. Preheat the oven to 180C and mix the self-raising flour, baking powder and butter in a bowl using your hands.

2. Add in the cheese, as well as the chopped wild garlic leaves and then the milk. Combine all ingredients together to make a soft dough. Use a food mixer to combine together as this makes the dough easier to work with I find.

3. Spread a little dusting of flour onto a clean work surface, turn out the dough and knead it gently before making it into a round shape about 2 cm thick.

4. Using a scone cutter, cut out your shapes, until all the dough has been used.

5. Place each scone on a floured baking tray, be sure they are evenly spread apart from one another – you may need two baking trays. Bake in the oven for 12-14 minutes or until golden brown. Best served warm slathered with butter.

Spring suppers. Wild garlic pesto instantly transforms a bowl of pasta or a puff pastry tart, topped with asparagus and chives.

Blackberries

I have many fond memories stomping along hedgerows on my parents' farm as a child, picking blackberries. To this day, I still feel like a child when I find myself bounding through the woods or along the back lanes of our house, trying to find a good stash of beautiful blackberries to dine on. Often, few make it back to the kitchen. A common theme running throughout this book.

This childhood favourite is now enjoyed by my own children, who, like me, love filling their mouths full of freshly picked blackberries, especially on the walk home from school. Purple-stained fingers and faces are not only a sign of a good walk but also a sign the days are getting shorter, and winter is creeping ever closer. You will be guaranteed a plentiful supply between August and September but remember long sleeved tops, trousers and gloves are recommended as although these autumnal jewels are delicious, they are a little prickly.

Fun fact. Blackberries picked near to the sea along coastal paths have a distinct salty sea taste to them. Give them a go and give your taste buds a blast. Blackberries also come from the same family as roses, hence the same prickly nature of both plants.

Top tip. Blackberries work well in savoury dishes. Try roasting them alongside other autumnal gems like pumpkin, apples, and parsnips.

Waste not, want not. Like raspberries, blackberries also freeze well and hold on to their flavour and shape and don't turn too mushy when cooked. So, if you forage a big haul, freeze them in old ice cream tubs, add to your porridge or make into smoothies along with frozen banana, yoghurt and honey.

We spy blackberry

Blackberry meringue mess

An alternative to the traditional Eton mess, this 'recipe'
came about after a stomp up our back lane foraging
for blackberries and some meringue nests which were
snaffled into my shopping trolley by my youngest whilst I
wasn't paying attention. He's a sly one.

Again, not so much a recipe but a serving suggestion.
Break up 6 meringue nests into a bowl, fold through 6
large dollops of Greek yoghurt, a couple of handfuls of
blackberries and 2 tsp of runny honey. Divide between 4
ramekin dishes and finish with more fresh blackberries,
mint leaves and edible flowers.

Blackberry mini pies

Another easy peasy recipe for children to have a go at creating and another good reason to have a packet of puff pastry stashed in the fridge. They are also a great post-school snack when children are on the verge, and their tummies are rumbling. The sequel to this book should be one which revolves around using puff pastry as the foundation of any solid dish or 'Han-gry Recipes' to get you through the witching hours. Best attempt to finish this one first!

1. Begin by preheating the oven to 180C and roll out a packet of 350g shop-bought puff pastry onto a baking tray. The pastry normally comes with baking paper so no need for a dusting of flour.

2. Keep a quarter of the pastry for the lattices to go over the top of the pies and cut these into strips. Using a scone cutter, cut out as many mini pies as you can and place 2 tsp of fruit jam in the middle and 5 or 6 blackberries on top of the jam.

3. Place the pastry lattice strips on top and, using a pastry brush, gently brush a little milk over the top of the pastry.

4. Bake in the oven for 10-12 minutes or until golden brown.

100g butter

200g 70% dark chocolate cocoa solids

4 eggs

250g caster sugar

100g plain flour

1 tsp baking powder

30g cocoa

150g blackberries

Blackberry brownies

This is a bold statement, but this would be my desert island pudding option if I could take one with me. Chocolatey, gooey, moreish, and of course fruity, everything you could possibly want in a chocolate brownie and more.

1. Preheat the oven to 180C and line a 20 cm square tin with baking paper.

2. Melt the chocolate and butter in a bowl set over a pan of simmering water, or in a microwave on low. Stir every now and then.

3. Beat the eggs and sugar with an electric whisk until light and fluffy. Add in the cocoa powder, baking powder and flour until combined. Stir in the melted chocolate mixture.

4. Pour the brownie batter into the prepared tin, dot the blackberries on top. Bake for 20-25 minutes and leave to cool before cutting into the squares and demolishing in one sitting.

Elderflower

For a real taste and smell of summer, elderflower is a forager's favourite pick between May and June. The trees are found throughout the UK in woods, along roadsides and amongst hedgerows. They are ripe for the picking when there are lots and lots of tiny white flowers, which also have a sweet, summery scent.

You might be lucky enough to have your own elderflower tree in your garden or know of someone who does. In which case, it might be a red variety, which will give a pink tinge to any cordial that is made.

The flowers are edible once cooked but mildly toxic if eaten raw. Pick the flower heads on a dry, warm, and sunny day and give the heads a good shake to remove any bugs or beasties. To bottle both the taste and smell of summer, you will need a good basketful of the flower heads and then you will have the number one ingredient to make cordial and many other sweet treats.

Fun fact. Elderflower has an anti-inflammatory effect so is useful for respiratory infections. It is also a natural antihistamine. However, as with all natural remedies please consult your doctor before use.

Top tip. Elderflower cordial is not just for drinking but also lovely to drizzle over a very traditional Victoria sponge and let the summery flavours seep into it. Try also adding it to vanilla butter cream icing, for an extra summery blast.

30 elderflower heads

1.7litres boiling water

900g golden caster sugar

50g citric acid (available from most pharmacies)

3 lemons, sliced

Two good handfuls of non-sprayed fragrant rose petals (optional)

Lolly's N19 elderflower cordial

My niece Lolly is a creative genius in the kitchen. From a young age she has been making and creating and the results are delicious. Her garden in North London is a special place for our family, filled with memories from long summer days. Her garden is also home to a red elderflower tree, which means her elderflower cordial looks a little jazzier!

1. Give the elderflower heads a good shake to remove any little beasties, which might be taking cover.

2. Pour the boiling water over the sugar in a large pot and give it a good stir. Leave to cool.

3. Add in the citric acid, the lemon slices, and then the flowers and rose petals if using.

4. Leave in a cool place for 24 hours.

5. Strain through some muslin and transfer into sterilised bottles.

✳ We SPY ELderFLOWeR

Reduce, recycle, and grow...

Ideas to help you get recycling in the garden

No two growing spaces will ever be the same and I love that. We're all unique and our growing spaces should be too. What you decide to do with your space is entirely down to you and your creativity. When it comes to recycling in the garden, creativity knows no bounds. Your only limitation is your imagination. You can grow fruit, vegetables, and herbs as well as flowers in just about anything if you can safely make drainage holes in the bottom, using either a hammer and a nail or a drill.

By reusing and reviving old household items, which may otherwise have been thrown out, you are being kinder to the environment and also growing something new out of something old, as well as having fun.

These are just a few of our favourite upcycling projects. Give one or two ago.

1. Clean yoghurt cartons, tin cans, egg cartons, takeaway coffee cups, toilet roll tubes and plastic fruit tubs can all be used to make pots for sowing seeds in and then put on your windowsill to watch the magic happen.

2. We've all got an old pair of wellies lurking in a corner, which no longer keep your feet dry. Plant them up and give them a new lease of life. They're perfect for herbs and carrots. Tall adult wellies are great for growing sweet peas in too, just add a long stick so the plant can climb onwards and upwards.

3. Watering cans, coal buckets and bread bins look great with flowers grown in them and are an interesting talking point if placed at your front door. We found all three in the cellar of our house when we moved in just before lockdown, so, of course, we re-purposed them.

4. Cattle troughs are also an excellent statement if space allows and can often be found on Gumtree – or approach a friendly farmer. In the spring, we planted a bulb lasagne of daffodils, tulips and wallflowers on top too. Then it's all change and we'll remove the bulbs and grow sunflowers, dahlias, and cosmos to see us through the summer months and into autumn.

5. Wicker gift baskets can also be reused and are good for growing lettuce and salad leaves. If they're lined with plastic, just pierce a few holes in the bottom for drainage.

6. I sourced an old wheelbarrow from a local bargaining website. I gave them seeds and chicken wire and I got a brand new plant pot of sorts. We drilled a few extra holes into its base and turned it into a tomato and basil planter. It's also become a great herb planter.

7. We grow so many pumpkin plants and although I give some away, I don't have the heart to part with them all as you become quite attached! Having used up all our pots and containers, I dug out an old baby bath, drilled some holes in the base and grew one of the smaller varieties of pumpkin, 'Jack Be Little', in it.

8. Again, we had far too many courgette plants, but I love courgettes, so we used the sink of our mud kitchen and removed the plug hole for drainage. Voilà! It was hugely successful. In the autumn, we plant it up with tulips and daffodil bulbs and winter pansies on top.

Top; Our mud kitchen sink made for a pretty good growing space for one of our courgette plants, when running low on containers.

Bottom; This old wheelbarrow was given a new lease of life. We turned it essentially into a salad bowl and grew salad leaves, basil plants, calendula flowers and a tomato plant and have also grown herbs in it to transform mealtimes.

Let's go wild! How to create a buzz about bees and other wildlife in your garden...

Nature at the heart of our gardens

In terms of garden exposure, I grew up at a time when beautiful, yet formal rose gardens, pristine lawns and manicured borders fit to burst with perfect rows of annual bedding plants were the order of the day.

However, I have long been drawn to the wilds of nature, whether that be the rugged Scottish southwest coast where I grew up or the moors of the Southern Upland Way. There is a wonder and curiosity about nature, which children are naturally drawn too. Even if this wonder and interest falls by the wayside after their childhood ends, there is a fighting chance, due to this early exposure, that they will be drawn back to nature and in turn make an effort to protect it.

Having grown up on a farm surrounded by so much unspoilt countryside, I naturally find myself drawn to green spaces, looking for new life in the shape of bees, butterflies, birds and so much more. This feeling is even stronger in urban settings, where wildlife and nature are so important, but so often have to fight for survival with concrete driveways and fake grass – suffocating new life and intrigue.

Wildlife should be at the heart of every garden and green space, and we need to garden with and for nature, resisting the urge to chop, mow and spray for the sake of appearance. Wild can be and is beautiful. Even a patch of nettles in a garden has its benefits, as a host plant for butterfly larvae and vital food for insects.

As we navigate our way forward, gardening and how we approach our green spaces should be about embracing colour, gardening in a way that supports biodiversity and allows it to thrive and take centre stage. We should garden and grow sustainably. By doing this Mother Nature can breathe easily and do her job and we can enjoy her beauty without causing further harm to an already fragile environment.

Bees, butterflies, and other garden insects not only pollinate but provide theatre and therapy within a garden. Without wildlife, Mother Nature is suppressed. If we continue on the dangerous path we have been driving along for some time, extracting peat, continuing to use single-use plastic, not recycling or re-purposing and using pesticides, Mother Nature will turn against us.

The warning signals have been fired, summers are becoming increasingly hotter and drier, winters milder and rain fall heavier. As guardians of our green spaces, we must prioritise planet-friendly gardening. Not necessarily great swathes of wildflower meadows and overgrown grasses waist-high, but patches of wildflowers and colourful perennials – attracting pollinators, and shrubs, providing food for birds in the winter. Planting different species of trees and hedgerows instead of fences will provide food, shelter, and space for nesting birds, while water in a garden is not only good for our mental health but also for wildlife.

A man-made crisis has evolved, and biodiversity is vanishing as a result. The footprints we make on nature as we step forward must be positive. I witnessed a glimmer of hope during the pandemic and never before has climate change been hurled into the spotlight in such a way as it was during COP 26 in 2021. However, this appetite needs harnessing. We require more action, less talking and we need the people who fell in love with their green spaces in the summer of 2020 to hold on to this love.

When I asked my eldest son what COP 26 was all about, as it was taking place on our doorstep and very much the hot topic in the classroom, the then six-year-old replied "Well mum, you see the leaders of the world are all coming to Glasgow. They are going to try to sort out the fight which man has been having with Mother Nature." He was spot on.

I don't have all the answers to sort out this man-made catastrophe swirling around us, but I do know gardening is not just a hobby but is something for the greater good now and for our future. We need to put our green fingers to good use to make a difference and change the tide.

Buzzing about bees

Bees play an important role, not only as pollinators but also by attracting and engaging interest in vital garden insects. They are the gatekeepers, sparking interest and intrigue into our garden ecosystems, which need protected and preserved. I have yet to meet a child who doesn't share my fascination and love with bees.

Bees are vital to our food security. It's no secret that bees and other pollinators, including moths, butterflies, hoverflies, and wasps are in decline, with the number of wild bees declining by a quarter since 1990. Pollinators are fundamental to the rich tapestry of life. Without them what we cook in our kitchens and serve on our plates would look very different. One in every three mouthfuls of food depends on pollination. Bees pollinate flowers, fruit, and vegetables, helping them to grow by transferring pollen between the male and female parts of flowers. This in turn allows the plants to grow seeds and fruit. A staggering 90% of wild plants and 75% of crops depend on animal pollination.

While managed honeybees are not at risk currently, the big concern is for wild bees, which pollinate many of the crops we consume daily. There is only one domesticated honeybee but there are a staggering 20,000 varieties of wild bees and it is these bees that are the key cog in our food supply. Without them, our environment would look very different.

Why are they in decline? Several factors but largely due to habitat loss, pollution, pesticides, and climate change. Wildflower meadows and other species of rich grasslands, once a normal part of the natural landscape, have been destroyed. Nearly 7.5 million acres of wildflower meadows have been lost since the 1930s. We may not be able to re-wild to the same extent, but much can be done in our communities, schools, and back gardens to make a difference.

Bees are not the only insect under threat. There are many more garden insects – playing a pivotal role in the pollination process. However, I guess bees have long captured our imagination and interest. You could say they are the poster boy/girl for the world of insects if you like. We need to hold on to that interest amongst children and adults alike, widen and grow it.

Now more than ever before, there has been much chatter about re-wilding and sustainable gardening, with good reason. In the UK alone, it's estimated there are 30 million gardeners. That's a lot of people power to make a huge positive difference to the environment if we gardened with the planet in mind and embraced our wilder sides. For a long time, neat, tidy edges and sharp, short lawns have been the order of the day and if a strand of grass was left to go astray, you might have been seen as untidy by the neighbours. However, who cares what Mr Jones over the fence thinks? I should add my neighbours are lovely, as are their gardens.

This is a hangover from the Victorian period when lawnmowers were viewed as a status symbol and lawns as perfect as Wimbledon's Centre Court were the aim. Not anymore. Letting your grass grow a little, cutting it less, or not at all for the month of May, and beyond, while letting things go wild, is beneficial for biodiversity. If you're following a rigid gardening plan and trying to keep things tidy, less mowing reduces stress and pressure and gives you more time to sit back, relax and enjoy what you have created. Let the buttercups, dandelions and daisies take their place in your garden and watch the bees and butterflies' circle.

We need to shake off the straight jacket of gardening past and embrace a wilder version. Tear up the rule book and garden with wildlife at the centre of everything we do. Bundles of twigs and leaves and long, luscious grass is okay and will captivate a greater interest in gardening, especially amongst children. Plant another tree if space allows and go wild for colour and variety. Remember, an unruly and untidy garden is a kinder garden. The bees and all garden wildlife will love you forever more. Colour, biodiversity, and sustainability should be our three main focuses when it comes to our gardens and green spaces.

BUZZIN ABOUT BEES

1. Bees have four wings.

2. Honeybees have a dance called the waggle dance, which is how they communicate about where to find food.

3. All worker bees are female.

4. In her whole lifetime a bee will produce 1/12 of a teaspoon of honey.

5. To produce 1kg of honey, bees will fly the distance of three times around the world.

6. Bees love variety, and they love the colour blue.

7. The type of flower that the bee takes nectar from also determines what the honey will taste like.

8. The queen bee can produce 2,000 eggs a day.

9. If a bee stings you, it will die.

10. The male bee, which is also known as the drone, has bigger eyes so it can go in search of the queen bee.

The meadows in Linn Park in Glasgow are alive with wildlife.

Be a Dandelion Lover

Dandelions are considered by many to be a weed and a bit of a nuisance. However, I am on the campaign trail, to persuade you to look at dandelions a little more favourably.

1. Dandelions provide insects with an early source of nectar.

2. Their wide-spreading roots loosen hard-packed soil and aerate the earth. The deep taproot pulls nutrients such as calcium from deep in the soil for other plants to use.

3. Every part of the dandelion can be used. Blanch the leaves to add to salads, the roots make a type of 'coffee', and the flowers can be used to make salves, soaps, oils, vinegars, and teas.

4. The word dandelion comes from 'dent de lion', which is French for lions tooth. They are named after lions, because of their lion tooth shaped leaves.

5. They have been around for a very long time, used by Egyptians, Greeks, and Romans, and in traditional Chinese medicine. Before the 20th century they were embraced for their beauty and used as a source of food and medicine.

6. What child doesn't love blowing the seed head to remove all the seeds to find out if their secret crush loves them or loves them not? I know I certainly did!

A bold statement but *nasturtiums*, might just be one of my favourite flowers in the garden. Bold, bright and brash, they are beautiful nuggets of gold in the garden, successfully self-seeding to provide an abundance of colour every year, right up to the first frost.

As well as bringing a smile to your face, nasturtiums are hardworking, useful and delicious.

1. The flowers are edible and can be used in salads and to decorate cakes.

2. The leaves are also edible and like the flowers have a peppery taste and can be used in salads and made into pesto.

3. The seeds if collected early can be pickled to make what is commonly known as 'poor man's capers'.

4. As they are prolific self-seeders you can collect the seeds and store them to gift to friends and family. A great addition to a seed sale.

5. They are also a great addition to a vegetable patch as nasturtiums make for great companion plants. The flowers attract pollinators including bees, butterflies, and hoverflies, while they also keep pesky beasties away from your crops. What's more, they also attract aphids, so by growing nasturtiums alongside your vegetables, the aphids will eat the nasturtiums, rather than ruin your harvest.

10 simple steps to make a wilder greener space.

1. Open your doors to butterflies, moths, bees, and hoverflies by setting up a 'Nectar Cage'. Plant a range of plants which will flower throughout the year; buddleia, echinacea, marigolds, English bluebells, hyacinth, honeysuckle, verbena, anemone, sunflowers, lavender, cat mint, rosemary, chives, snowdrops, daffodils, allium, cosmos, foxgloves, helenium, lupins, poppies, and nasturtiums.

2. Every school, nursery, community garden and home needs a bug hotel. It's a great construction project for every one of every age with no need for planning permission! Look to use recycled material such as old pallets, bricks, tin cans and broken terracotta pots, as well as leaves, twigs, branches, and pinecones. You could make a smaller version from five tin cans, glued together, and tied with garden twine around the middle. Fill each can with twigs and pinecones and hang on a fence.

3. As autumn creeps up on us, there is a huge urge to get outside, and tidy everything up, pulling up annuals, removing seed heads and lifting every leaf and twig in sight. There's a reason we say a wilder garden is a kinder garden. Not only does it reduce your workload, but you are helping local wildlife. So rather than dismantling all your sunflowers, leave some to loom large and provide food for birds. Piles of leaves, twigs and cuttings are great habitats for hedgehogs in search of shelter.

4. If each of us planted a tree and a hedgerow, we would be helping the fight against climate change and provide habitats and food for wildlife.

5. Throughout the year, especially during the colder months when food is scarce, be sure to hang bird feeders. Provide them with high energy seeds, nuts, and fat balls to keep hunger at bay and clean the bird feeders regularly. This is also a great activity to do with children and you can keep a diary, making a note of regular visitors. Birds are also vital for keeping things in check and will eat insects including every gardener's nemesis the dreaded slug, which might otherwise nibble on your lettuces. Common birds to look out for include robins, blackbirds, blue tits, chaffinches, and magpies.

6. Water not only helps us to relax, but a source of water is also important to attract wildlife to our green spaces. You don't need a big space to create a pond. Simply make a hole in the ground, submerge an old washing tub into the hole and let it fill up with rainwater.

7. Don't be a slave to the lawnmower. Let the grass grow and let the bees and the butterflies come to feast as the dandelions, clover, buttercups, and daisies emerge. Reduce the number of times you cut your grass or simply leave an area of grass, which

you don't cut at all. It will become an 'all you can eat' buffet bonanza for bees and insects of all shapes and sizes.

8. Embrace weeds. They are after all, as the saying goes, simply flowers in the wrong place. Unless, of course, they are invasive weeds such as Japanese knotweed or bindweed or couch grass, in which case remove them by the roots before they take hold of the rest of your garden and strangle it.

9. Stop using pesticides. There really is no need and it is a sure-fire way to reduce the number of visitors in your garden. It's all about balance and letting go of the need to control everything. Remember, gardens and green spaces are part of a much bigger picture, which we are here to protect and preserve, not destroy. We are, after all, just the guardians. We need to work with Mother Nature not against her. This is where companion planting comes into its own and makes for a much more interesting and lively growing space. Nasturtiums, calendula, marigolds, and sunflowers are excellent companion plants, especially when growing vegetables.

10. I've said it already, but I'll say it again, use peat-free compost or, better still, if space allows, start making your own compost.

The humble sunflower.
A bee's best friend.

Top left to right. Crocus, poppy, cornflower, achillea, primula, lavender, single rose, rudbekia, and allium.

Top left to right. Buddleia, aster, marigold, nasturtium, single dahlia, helenium, sunflower, cosmos, and calendula. All of these flowers are loved by pollinators.

We need to garden with nature, rather than against it. The results will be far more satisfying, with more life, more colour and more interest in every nook and cranny, no matter how big or small our green space is.

Honey

I couldn't write about bees and wildlife and not include a few recipes featuring the liquid gold that is honey. I think you'll agree recipes with honey as the star ingredient may be more appetising than snail porridge or frogs' legs on toast with deep-fried slugs on the side. Although we are in Glasgow, and it has been said, if you go into a chippy in Glasgow, they will deep-fry anything!

Good quality honey is a precious thing. A lot of hard work goes into each teaspoon. In an average bee's lifetime, it will make just one twelfth of a teaspoon of honey. You'll not be leaving any on your toast, knowing that fact now, will you? The flavour also depends on the flower species from which the bees gather the nectar. In cities such as London, often thought as a sprawling concrete jungle, there are hives aplenty and the bees in the capital are feasting on a rich and diverse flora diet from rooftop gardens, as well as trees and great swathes of parks, with which the city is awash.

However, the big problem beekeepers in the UK are faced with is cheap, imported honey. This is having a devastating economic impact on UK beekeepers. This is also the reason you will come across honey in the supermarket for as low as 69 pence.

A lot of the pollen has been removed and jars are bulked out with sugar syrup. The UK is the world's biggest importer of Chinese honey, which is one sixth of the price of honey produced by bees in Britain and is often a blend of different honeys from non-EU countries. One of my favourite suppliers is The Scottish Bee Company and its honey says what it is on the jar, and is made with people and the environment in mind. It is authentic with no added sugar syrup and no cheap honey mixed in.

The take home message is always read the label and don't reach for the cheaper jars of honey on the supermarket shelves. The same goes for all food products, especially our dairy and meat. We have great producers and farms who take a huge amount of pride in their work and the health and welfare of their livestock and the environment is at the heart of everything they do.

HONEY
BEE

350g porridge oats

225g unsalted butter

75g dark soft brown sugar

6 tbsp honey

The zest of half an orange

2 tsp chopped thyme

Orange and thyme honey flapjacks

Everyone needs a good flapjack recipe up their sleeve, and it is one of the first recipes many children learn to bake themselves. Better than any shop-bought bars, these flapjacks are a must for lunch boxes and a great emergency snack when everyone is feeling just a little 'han-gry' – myself included.

1. Preheat the oven to 180C and line a small baking tray with paper.

2. In a pan on a low heat on the hob, gently melt together the butter and the sugar, making sure it doesn't stick to the bottom or burn. Then stir in the honey.

3. Add the porridge oats to a large mixing bowl and then add in the honey mixture, combining everything together.

4. Next add the orange zest and thyme.

5. Spread the mixture into the prepared baking tray and bake for 15 to 20 minutes. Leave to cool completely before cutting into squares. I know this will be tricky, but please do. It will be worth the wait for the sweet sticky goodness to come.

375g porridge oats

100g dessicated coconut

30g pumpkin seeds

30g sunflower seeds

50ml rapeseed oil

150ml honey

125g cranberries and raisins

2 tsp mixed spice

Cranberry and coconut granola

Granola is one of those things I would happily eat for breakfast, lunch, and supper. Although I'm not sure how balanced a diet that would be. Nevertheless, just like the flapjacks in the recipe before, it's tasty and super easy to whisk up yourself and, unlike the shop-bought stuff, a lot cheaper. In the run up to Christmas, it makes for a lovely homemade gift too – if you can bring yourself to part with it.

1. Preheat the oven to 160C.

2. Put the oats, coconut, pumpkin, and sunflower seeds into a big bowl and then pour in the honey and rapeseed oil. Combine everything together and stir in the mixed spice.

3. Spread the granola mixture over baking paper on a large baking tray and bake in the oven for 35 minutes, giving it a stir halfway through.

4. Leave to cool on the side before mixing in the cranberries and raisins and then store in an airtight container before scoffing for breakfast or for pudding with yoghurt and berries.

About the author

A farmer's daughter from the southwest coast of Scotland, Helen is a storyteller who is passionate about food, horticulture, and farming. While she will always be a country girl at heart, as a city dweller since leaving home at the age of 17 she is driven to encourage more communities and families to grow their own and cook seasonally. Not to become self-sufficient but to uncover the health and environmental benefits that come from gardening and cooking seasonally. With a history of her own mental health problems for over 20 years Helen has sought huge solace from her own green space and recognises the power that gardening, and nature can have to help people both physically and mentally, something she champions daily.

Not a trained chef or horticulturist, Helen is a good old fashioned home cook with a degree in history specialising in European feminism! She married a rugby player who unsurprisingly, despite being retired, still has a very healthy appetite and with three boys a lot of time is spent as a family in the kitchen cooking and making a mess. While also writing, and keeping her family on the straight and narrow, she also hosts the podcast, "Grow, Cook, Inspire" and teaches children to garden, grow, cook and be a little more wild.

Useful resources

www.rhs.org.uk

www.charlesdowding.co.uk

www.sarahraven.co.uk

www.suttons.co.uk

www.jparkers.co.uk

www.plantgrow.co.uk

www.calaedonianhorticulture.co.uk

www.soilassociation.org

www.mind.org.uk

www.breathingspace.scot

www.samaritans.org

***

Some of Ruth's beautiful images throughout the book can also be coloured in. Perfect for a rainy day.

Acknowledgements

Admittedly I didn't think I would get to this page, but here I am. Writing my first book was never going to be an easy ride. However, throw in a global pandemic, three small children, as well as all of life's ups and downs, and an enormous dollop of imposter syndrome, I can testify not only was it not an easy ride, but it was also a rather tumultuous ride.

What started as an idea at the start of lockdown from my friend and neighbour Ruth, has resulted in the creation of this book. Thank you, Ruth, for keeping the faith and for your beautiful illustrations, which bring the book alive. To James, thank you for steering the ship out of the harbour at the very beginning and guiding me with your expert knowledge.

To Lucy and Russ, thank you for giving me the confidence to get back on the horse and letting my creative side shine brighter than it ever has. I will forever be obsessed with pumpkins.

To all my friends and family, for your patience and for listening to me go on and on and for allowing me to bounce ideas and recipes off you and bombard you with gluts of courgettes and pumpkins. Eileen and Adam, thank you for your unwavering support, eagle eyes and phenomenal attention to detail and above all your good humour and friendship. To Ally, you really have helped to drive my love of all things gardening, not to mention plant pots.

Lucy, Mandy, and Heather thank you for your time and patience, editing, proof reading and designing. Self-publishing has been a whole new ball game, so to have your skill set has been invaluable. Rhiannon, thank you for your support and wisdom at the beginning.

Geoff, thank you for letting me take over the garden, dig it all up and grow vegetables and flowers. I love you lots! Otto, Reuben, and Ivor, this book is for you. I hope I have sown a lifelong love for nature, plants, gardening, and cooking.

Finally, if this book inspires just one new gardening club or one child to start sowing seeds and to be a little bit wilder, I will be happy.